FRAGMENTS OF TIME

(MEMOIRS)

SNIGDHA AGRAWAL

Made with ♥ on the Notion Press Platform
www.notionpress.com

To my beloved late parents, Anila and Biswanath Banerjee...

This book is dedicated to you in profound gratitude for the foundation you built with your love, patience and sacrifices. Your wisdom, encouragement and belief in me have been my guiding light and have shaped me into the person I am today. You taught me that success is achieved through drive, dedication, and determination. Your legacy continues to inspire every step I take. Your love remains a constant presence in my life and I carry it with me always.

Contents

Preface

Introduction

Writing a memoir is an act of preservation—of memories, emotions, and the lessons learned along life's winding journey. This collection of stories offers not a complete portrait but rather a mosaic of moments that have shaped who I am. Some memories are vivid, etched in my mind as if they occurred yesterday, while others are gentler, like a distant hum. Yet, each one has left an indelible mark on my soul.

In these pages, you won't find a neat, linear narrative. Life rarely unfolds in such a way. Instead, this memoir reflects life's twists and turns, its unexpected detours and the quiet revelations that define our shared human experience. There are stories of joy and laughter, days of sorrow and loss, moments of uncertainty and glimpses of hope. Together, these threads weave the larger fabric of my existence.

This book is not only about me. It is also a tribute to the people who have touched my life, the places that grounded me and the experiences that broadened my perspective. By sharing these personal moments, I hope they resonate with you, the reader. Perhaps you'll find fragments of your own journey in mine or draw comfort and inspiration from the lessons I've learned along the way.

As you turn these pages, I hope that you feel a sense of connection—not only to my story but to your own and the stories of those around you. Because, in the end, life is a collection of stories: ones we carry, ones we pass down and ones that shape how we see the world.

When I first considered writing my memoir, a series of questions came to mind. Would readers find inspiration in these stories? Perhaps not. At best, I thought, my audience might be limited to my immediate family and close friends. But then I reminded myself that memoirs are not necessarily written for the masses. Instead, they are a testament to a life lived—a way to honour the experiences, emotions, and milestones that make us who we are.

At seventy-plus, I can confidently say that my life has been fulfilling. Like everyone, I've faced storms and enjoyed moments of calm. On the balance sheet of life, the scales have tilted towards the positive. My motivation for writing stems from a desire to leave a legacy for my children, grandchildren and future generations—a glimpse into a life they may never fully understand but can still connect with. History may overlook the seemingly insignificant events that were monumental to me, but perhaps these stories will offer insight into the person I was.

This is not about grand achievements or seeking fame. It is about showing that a life was lived—a life that mattered in its quiet, unassuming way. As Maya Angelou wisely said, "If you're going to live, leave a legacy. Make a mark on the world that can't be erased." Writing this memoir is my way of leaving that mark, of saying, "I was here, and this is my story."

The Memoir-Writing Process

Writing a memoir is unlike other forms of storytelling. It doesn't require elaborate plotting, the invention of imaginative characters, or tying up every loose end. Instead, it is an opportunity to reflect on the past, put memories into words, and create vivid images for readers. The process is deeply personal and immensely rewarding—especially if it encourages readers to journey through its chapters and in the end, reflect with a quiet thought: "In the ordinariness of her life, I found fragments of connection."

Of course, the process is not without its challenges. There's an inherent vulnerability in sharing one's innermost thoughts and struggles. Fear creeps in: Will this resonate with anyone? Is my story significant enough? These doubts are natural, but they are outweighed by the profound satisfaction of seeing a life story come together on the page, bare and honest.

A Legacy of Connection

Through this memoir, I hope to achieve more than simply documenting my journey. I wish to spark moments of connection, reminding readers of the shared experiences that bind us all. Whether you are a family member, a friend, or someone encountering my story for the first time, I hope that these pages inspire reflection, understanding, and perhaps even a deeper appreciation for your own journey.

Because, in the end, this is what life is about—a collection of stories that touch, teach and connect us across generations. This memoir is my story, my legacy, and my way of leaving behind a mark that says: I lived, and I lived well.

— Snigdha Agrawal

Acknowledgements

As I reflect on the journey of writing this memoir, I am overwhelmed with gratitude for the people who have stood by me, offering their love, support and encouragement along the way.

First and foremost, my deepest thanks go to my partner. Your unwavering belief in me, boundless patience, and steadfast support have been a constant source of strength and inspiration.

To my late parents, whose wisdom, values and love laid the foundation of my life—I owe everything to you. And to my only surviving sibling, thank you for being my steadfast ally, a source of unconditional support and understanding.

To my dear friends, both old and new, I am grateful for your presence in my life. You have reminded me of the beauty of shared experiences and the strength of community. You have been my sounding board, anchor, and inspiration.

Lastly, to you, the reader—thank you, for taking the time to journey through these pages. It is my heartfelt hope that these stories resonate with you, that you find threads of connection in them and perhaps even a reflection of your own experiences.

With deep and abiding gratitude,

Snigdha Agrawal

Declaration

Author's Note

This memoir is a reflection of my personal feelings, observations and impressions, which may differ from how others perceive and relate to the same experiences.

While memoir writing is a deeply personal endeavour, it also demands a commitment to respect the privacy and dignity of those who appear within its pages. To honour this responsibility, I have taken care to protect the identities of individuals by altering names and details when necessary. Real names of places or people are included only when they are already part of the public domain.

I intend to present my truth with honesty and integrity while safeguarding the trust and confidentiality of others. I ask readers to approach this memoir with an open mind, recognizing that personal experiences are inherently subjective and filtered through the lens of memory.

As the saying goes, "The best memories don't have evidence beyond the picture in the mind." The stories I share here are deeply rooted in my recollections, shaped by the unique prism of my own life.

— Snigdha Agrawal

Disclaimer

The images presented in this book have been generated through AI-based prompts and are not subject to copyright protection. These images are created exclusively for this book and are intended solely to enhance and complement the narratives contained herein. They are not part of the copyrighted content of this book, which applies strictly to the written material.

CHAPTER ONE

Birth and Infancy

Two daughters laugh, their voices bright
Now twin girls join, a double light
Four hearts that bloom, a perfect blend
Parent's joy, that knows no end
In every smile, in every song
love grows deep, forever strong
With four daughters now, their world is complete
A harmony, so pure, so sweet

The following account is a reconstruction of my earliest years, from birth to age four—a time for which I have scant or no personal memories. It is based on fragments of hearsay, faded photographs, imaginative embellishments and a good deal of contextual interpretation. The narrative has been pieced together from family conversations, with names altered to protect privacy.

In the not-so-bustling city of Calcutta, the year 1952 ushered in the monsoons with their usual fervour. The air hung heavy with the smell of wet earth, and the rhythmic pitter-patter of rain echoed through the narrow, winding streets. In a modest, middle-class home tucked away on a quiet lane in Dum Dum, the family's focus was fixed on Shobita's third pregnancy.

She was carrying big this time, enduring an uncomfortable and trying third trimester. Already the mother of two daughters—Shilpi, aged nine, and Sanchita, aged seven—Shobita was fervently hoping for a son. A boy, after all, would not only complete the family but also bring a sense of societal approval that a daughter often couldn't. In a community steeped in the unspoken preference for male heirs, Shobita felt the weight of expectations pressing down on her, even in her moments of rest.

Her husband, Bhuban, remained a quiet observer. Though he rarely voiced his thoughts, who could say if he didn't share similar hopes? Perhaps he, too, wished for a son—a child who could carry on the family name, inherit responsibilities, and solidify their standing within a judgmental society.

Bhuban's mother, the matriarch of the family, sat in the corridor outside the OT, her face set with lines of expectation. She had long awaited the birth of a grandson who would carry on the family name, a son who would become the pride of the household. The family doctor, an elderly gentleman, had arrived earlier in the evening, his medical bag in hand, prepared to help deliver the child.

Hours later, after a tense and difficult labour, the first cries of a baby filled the hospital corridor. Relief washed over everyone. "It's a girl," the doctor said, his voice heavy with an unspoken understanding. Bhuban wondered why. And before Mother and Son could dwell on it, another cry pierced the air.

"Another one!" the doctor exclaimed. The surprise of the birth of twins caught everyone off guard. And as the second baby was delivered, it too was a girl.

Two more daughters.

"Two more girls..." Shobita muttered, still groggy under the effect of heavy sedation. She was overwhelmed with love cradling her newborn daughters. The feeling of inadequacy never entered her mind, with the addition of two more girls. She knew Bhuban never expressed his preference for boys over girls. But knew what her mother-in-law was thinking. Bhuban stood by the door, gazing at his wife and the newborns. Daughters. The smile on his face spoke volumes.

When news of the birth of the twin girls was announced to the older girls, there was pandemonium. "Let's go see them", rushing and tripping over each other in entering the room where their mother was confined for the next few days. Their eyes widened at the sight of the tiny, wriggling babies wrapped in soft cloths. "They're so small!" whispered Shilpi, her voice filled with awe. Sanchita ever the protector, reached out gently and touched one of the baby's cheeks. "We're big sisters now," she said softly, more to herself than to anyone else.

Shobita, her exhaustion briefly forgotten, smiled weakly at her elder daughters. "Yes, you are. You must help me take care of them."

The grandmother chose to embrace the situation with grace. The day after the twins returned home, she gathered the family for a simple naming ceremony. A staunch believer in tradition, she took charge of the rituals and selected names for the girls. The fairer twin was named Shuili, after the white flower with an orange stem that symbolized purity, while the darker twin was named Krishna.

However, Bhuban voiced his disagreement. "Ma, you're being colour-biased," he remarked, challenging his mother's choices; a reflection on a long-standing practice of naming babies according to their skin tones. This prompted a reconsideration and Krishna's name was changed to Shefali—a name that, like Shuili, also referred to the same flower. By renaming Krishna to Shefali, Bhuban not only sought to honour her individuality but also to challenge the subtle yet pervasive notion that beauty and worth are intrinsically linked to colour. In this small act of defiance, the family took a step towards acknowledging and addressing societal biases deeply entrenched in minds.

The ceremony was small, just family and a few close friends. Despite the muted celebrations, Shilpi and Sanchita were thrilled. They didn't care about the whispers of disagreement or the subdued mood of the adults. They had new sisters to care for and they were determined to do so.

As the weeks passed, Shilpi and Sanchita took to their new roles with enthusiasm. While their mother was recovering and their grandmother was busy with household duties, the elder girls became the de facto caretakers of their baby sisters. Sanchita, with her quiet maturity, rocked the babies to sleep, singing lullabies in her sweet, melodic voice. Shilpi, with her boundless energy, would make faces and coo at the twins, trying to make them laugh.

Bhuban watched his daughters grow closer and though he still felt the weight of societal expectations, there was a certain tenderness that softened his heart. Slowly, he began to accept that his family of four daughters was his blessing, even if it wasn't what his mother had expected.

One evening, as the twins lay asleep and the rains outside had softened to a gentle drizzle, Shobita watched her four girls closeted together and felt an overwhelming love and quiet pride. At that moment, she realized that her family was complete, just as it was. And in time, so did everyone else.

As the months passed, the house in Dum Dum, Calcutta, came alive with the joyful noise and activity of four growing daughters. The twins thrived under the tender care of their elder sisters. They were inseparable, often found curled up together in a handcrafted cradle made by their grandmother, their tiny hands intertwined, as if they couldn't bear to be apart. Their innocence and soft giggles filled the house with an undeniable warmth. The twins' synchronized smiles, their big, curious eyes and their uncanny ability to sense when their older siblings were near added a special magic to the household.

As the years passed, the bond between the four sisters grew stronger. Shilpi, now twelve, took on the role of a second mother, always watching over her younger siblings with a protective eye. She was patient and nurturing and pitched in with kitchen chores, often helping her mother prepare meals or tending to her sisters' needs. Sanchita, ever playful and full of life, entertained the twins with stories, games and singing to them, her voice echoing through the house.

Soon the twins began to show their unique personalities, one quiet and observant, the other bursting with energy, running, and exploring. One bottle-fed, the other breast-fed. Not out of choice, but compulsion following the doctor's advice to be bottle-fed with a special brand of infant milk. Shiuli was diagnosed with jaundice, very early on in her life, raising concerns for the entire family.

Despite the differences, the four girls were inseparable. They spent their afternoons playing in the courtyard, making up imaginary worlds where they were the heroines of grand adventures. In their world, there were no limits—only possibilities.

Bhuban often found himself watching his daughters with pride. Shilpi's quiet leadership, Sanchita's infectious joy, the hint of colour returning on Shuili's pale jaundiced complexion and Shefali's fearless spirit—they each brought something unique to the family. He realized that his daughters were more than enough.

The grandmother, now older and more fragile, would often sit on the veranda, watching her granddaughters with pride. "They are my legacy," she would say to herself, a smile playing on her lips.

And indeed, they were.

Following a job offer in 1956 Bhuban and his family moved out of Dum Dum to a gated community in the industrial belt of West Bengal and Bihar.

I often wondered if Baba ever felt disappointed about having four daughters—a nagging thought that lingered in my mind. Yet, I never dared to ask, fearing it might seem like questioning his unwavering love and devotion to us. Baba never expressed a desire for a son. Instead, he embraced his role as the only man in a household full of women with pride, as if he truly cherished the vibrant warmth and beautiful chaos that surrounded him.

My memories of our early years in Dum Dum are like whispers, fragile and elusive. I can stretch my recollection to reveal glimpses: a sturdy brick wall separating the two-storied house from a pond framed by coconut trees, the laughter of us girls echoing as we sat on bamboo mats spread on the grass, under the winter sun. I can almost feel the sunlight warming my skin at the recollection, the picture becoming sharper with the presence of a loyal black dog standing watch. His presence was a comforting shield as if he were our protector, our guardian.

Yet, I wonder if some of these images are merely reflections from childhood photos rather than actual memories. There are those grainy black-and-white images of us twins sprawled on a mat, the world around us a blur. It's fascinating to think about infantile amnesia—the way our minds can hold onto a few fleeting moments, while entire years slip through the cracks.

As I sift through the remnants of those days, my thoughts turn to another home—a bungalow with a wide balcony stretching across the front. I recall the gentle sway of the trees outside. Pixels woven into the fabric of my life. We moved there in 1956 when Baba secured a position with Bird & Company Ltd., a British firm deeply rooted in Calcutta, later nationalized by the Government of India.

In that new space, I could almost feel the excitement of change mingling with the bittersweet nostalgia for Dum Dum. It's a testament to how the threads of memory intertwine—each moment coloured by emotions, love and the ever-present question of belonging.

Childhood

From 1956 to 1968, our life felt like a fairy tale, cocooned in the safety of a gated community filled with people from various states and expats. A forgotten era, one that future generations would find hard to comprehend—a time of fun, freedom and an enveloping sense of security. Living in this community meant enjoying the comforts of huge furnished bungalows set on sprawling lawns, surrounded by flowering gardens. Perks included paid domestic staff, free electricity, fuel and transportation—benefits I was blissfully unaware of at the time.

Even after the lapse of more than five decades, the image of our bungalow remains vivid in my mind. It had four spacious rooms by today's standards and a large Puja room that doubled as storage.

The kitchen was decent-sized, complemented by a generous pantry and there were two bathrooms equipped with bathtubs, washbasins and wall cupboards. The bathroom doors had awning glass windows at the top which opened to release the accumulated odours of our bustling family of six—an early version of exhaust fans. During the sweltering summers, we often kept the windows open for ventilation, with two pedestal fans running constantly to combat the heat while we tended to our business. Baba took his own sweet time in the bathroom, treating the toilet like a throne where he could read 'The Statesman' (newspaper) from cover to cover while smoking his favourite cigarettes, leaving behind smoke clouds the next occupant had to deal with.

Running along the length of the house were two verandas—one in the front, broad and covered, spacious enough to double as a playground and a narrower, uncovered one at the back, perfect for hanging laundry. I remember some renovations that added two more rooms to the front veranda, trimming its size but still leaving enough space for us to stage plays, toss the tennikoit ring, and bat shuttlecocks to each other without seeing either fly over the railings.

Baba's wooden easy chair, with its broad armrests, held a place of honour on the veranda. From there, he had an unobstructed view of the golf course and the lush surroundings. I often wonder whether it was I or my twin who accidentally knocked over his glass of whiskey from the armrest during a wild attempt to catch the rubber ring—memory gets a bit fuzzy after six decades. What I do recall, though, is his gentle reminder to take our games outside. Naturally, we ignored it, continuing our antics on the balcony. One evening, as we played, a shuttlecock landed squarely on his head. We braced ourselves for a reprimand, but instead, he burst into laughter. The sound echoed through the house, a shared moment of joy that solidified our bond. He would sometimes abandon his chair to join the chaos, his own rule about playing outside conveniently forgotten as he tried to outdo us in tossing the ring. Rules, after all, were clearly meant to be broken—preferably with a good laugh and a flying tennikoit ring. Baba's patience and warmth made even the most chaotic moments feel like cherished memories.

In the children's bedroom, we slept on a king-size iron four-poster bed, shoulder to shoulder, leaving no room for our beloved *'pash balish'*—the side pillows we adored. We younger ones wedged between our older sisters, took liberties that would have made any sleep coach cringe. Our hands and legs flailed over their face, ribs, and thorax. Older sisters, indulgent by nature, never complained. Being seasoned babysitters, they knew how to roll with the chaos.

Some nights, we flopped into bed like exhausted puppies, barely able to keep our eyes open. My twin and I would look at our sisters with pleading eyes, silently begging them to do the nightly prayers for us— "*Om Namah Shivaya,*" (a Hindu mantra) to be chanted 108 times... their fingers doing that hypnotic counting thing our parents had drilled into us. To the soothing sound of their chant, we'd drift off into slumberland. After all, why deal with the finger movement when you can snooze through it like a tiny, divine sloth?

The next morning, Ma would come in to wake us for school and burst into laughter at the sight before her: four skewed heads on the bed. "*Bordi,*" the eldest sister, hanging precariously at the edge, teetering on the brink of disaster, *'Mejdi'*, the second oldest, curled up in a foetal position, trying to accommodate our little limbs. Ma always described us like circus performers caught mid-act, juggling for our lives—except the only thing we were juggling was sleep!

Storytelling was a nightly ritual in our household, and I had a particular fondness for spooky tales—the kind where *'bhoots'* (ghosts) raided the pantry to feast on *'narkel naru'* (coconut sweets) and mango *'murabba'* (sweet pickles) straight from their porcelain jars. One evening, *'Mejdi'* decided to weave an especially chilling tale.

“You know,” she began in a hushed tone, her voice dipping into an eerie cadence, “the late Mr Johnson—the man who lived in this house before us—had an insatiable sweet tooth. Even in death, he couldn’t resist sneaking into the pantry at night to indulge his cravings. If you’re very still, you might hear him crunching on Ma’s sweets—crunch... crunch... crunch.” She paused dramatically, her eyes narrowing to slits as she leaned closer.

“But beware,” she whispered, her tone dripping with foreboding, “never, ever disturb him during his midnight feast. They say if you do, he might mistake you for dessert!”

She wasn’t done. “Mr. Johnson loved reading too,” she continued. “Sometimes, you might find him in the drawing room, helping himself to Baba’s Agatha Christie novels. His spirit, they say, still clings to his habits in life”. That night, every creak of the old Bungalow, and every gust of wind brushing against the shutters seemed amplified, each sound mimicking the phantom footsteps of Mr Johnson, crunching away in the dark. I refused to set foot in the drawing room alone, convinced that his ghostly presence lingered there. In my mind’s eye, he was the quintessential British gentry: clad in a pinstriped suit with a waistcoat, a bowler hat perched atop his head, and soda glasses balanced on a hawk-like nose. His gaunt face, framed by the dim glow of the naked overhead bulb, seemed more spectral than the skeletons in my storybooks.

“If you ever have to go in after dark,” *Mejdi* added, her voice dropping to a conspiratorial whisper, “take a green chilli with you! It’ll send Mr. Johnson packing.” She claimed he had died of stomach ulcers after gorging on spicy Indian food. “Spice was his undoing in life, and it’s his weakness in death,” she concluded with a flourish.

I took her advice to heart. Whenever I needed to brave the drawing room, I clutched a green chilli tightly in my fist like a talisman. The trips were quick and frantic—a dash in to snatch a book from Baba's library, then a hurried escape to the safety of the veranda. My heart would race as if I had narrowly escaped his skeletal grasp. The cold, musty air of the drawing room only heightened my dread, and I would glance nervously over my shoulder, half-expecting to see his shadowy form emerge from behind Baba's chair.

Each encounter with the room felt like a brush with the paranormal, and the story of Mr. Johnson became an indelible part of my childhood's eerie imagination. Even as I grew older, the echo of *Mejdi's* tales lingered, ensuring that the drawing room never quite lost its ghostly aura.

By the time I turned ten, my sisters were packed off to boarding school, bringing an abrupt end to the ghost stories. The four-poster bed was sent to the factory shed, and we twins graduated to sleep on separate beds in our room. But the fear of encountering Mr Johnson lingered until we finally vacated the bungalow, which we believed to be haunted—an idea perpetuated by the older sisters' imaginative storytelling.

Now, as I write this with a smile, I think of my sisters, best friends until the end, resting in Heaven. Our family of six now shrunk to just two of us living in different states, and how time flies! Those childhood ghost stories stick in the mind like "stick jaw" (sticky candy) to teeth—hard to shake off.

And believe it or not, the habit of fighting over the 'pash balish' hasn't left. My husband and I sometimes find ourselves vying for the same pillow, usually after one of us unknowingly rolls it off the bed. "This is mine!" I assert, to which he replies, "No, it's mine, can't you see the impressions of my legs?" The inevitable blame game ensues, with sleepy protests and laughter echoing through the years, reminding us of those nights on the four-poster bed, lost in a world of memories and mischief.

Knocking on my memory door, I can clearly recall Mr. Murray, our next-door neighbour for a brief time. An old Britisher, he was a confirmed bachelor and a devout Christian, having once been a priest in his homeland. With his stern expression and lanky frame draped in suits that were two sizes too big, he reminded me of the imaginary Mr. Johnson I had conjured from childhood tales.

Mr. Murray mostly kept to himself, maintaining an air of mystery that intrigued us. His way of showing affection was unusual but endearing; he would send over generous portions of Shepherd's pie and caramel custard through his '*baburchi*' (cook) Bismillah. In return, Ma would whip up her famous '*kausha mangsho*' (spicy lamb curry), which he relished with gusto. I often wondered if he suffered from heartburn after those meals—eating rich, spicy food seemed risky for someone so solemn.

Fortunately, none of us were subjected to the unpleasant experience of smelling the sulfuric air that supposedly hung around his bedroom at night, as reported by his '*Baburchi*'. Our interactions were limited to the culinary exchanges, punctuated by polite nods when we crossed paths. What exactly his role was in the factory, I never discovered and why he accepted a job outside his home country, remains unanswered. Perhaps he harboured some unrequited love story, tucked away beneath that stern exterior.

In my imagination, he became a figure of intrigue—a character caught between two worlds, his past life as a priest haunting him like a ghost. The unspoken stories danced around us, filling our home with a mix of curiosity and caution. The mystery of Mr Murray lingered as a reminder of the lives I brushed against, yet never truly understood.

There were three factories in total, all housed within the gated community. A Steel factory, a Rolling Mill, and a Brick and fireclay factory, all subsidiaries of the parent company of Bird Group of companies, run and managed by the Britishers. Baba was employed in the steel factory in the Sales and Purchase Department. Later as the town evolved, somewhere in the early sixties, another factory McNally Bird Engineering Co. Ltd. came into existence, with modern housing complexes, changing the landscape from a sleepy British settlement into a mixture of the old and new. Gone was the golf course, gone were the tree-lined roads, and gone were the spaces where we raced full throttle and cycled without fear of being run down by speeding vehicles.

Beyond the habitable limits, were dense Sal forests with railway tracks cutting through them, carrying coal from one town to another, in this industrial belt across Bihar and West Bengal. During the summers, we kids woke up early to reach the tracks, to place one paisa copper coin (monetary unit of the rupee) on the railway tracks, waiting patiently for a train to pass. Retrieving the flattened misshapen coin, gave a kick of its own. Pure magic to young minds.

As the town expanded, more and more of those virgin forests were deforested and reclaimed for building modern housing complexes to accommodate the increasing factory staff. The volume of traffic also upped as more goods trucks entered to deliver raw materials for the factories. Uninterrupted view of the Sal forests that grew on the outer limits of the golf course, got obliterated.

One place that was left untouched, by urbanization, till I left, was the vicinity around the '*Khudiya*' River, a tributary of the '*Barakar*' River, meandering on the outskirts of the town. In summer, with the lowered water table, it was a sheer thrill wading bare feet in the shallow waters, with fishing nets, to catch the little silver fishes swimming, swirling, tickling our toes. The walk to the riverside was through forested slopes, home to the Santhals (tribals). Their villages rested on a flat tabletop on the steep river embankments. No one ever entered their territory. We did hear the beating of drums and drunken singing during festivals. It was rumoured that thieves and robbers roamed the forests and attacked the villagers, burning their homes and escaping with their valuables. Maybe, that was just to scare us away from making the riverside trips. I do, however, remember the howling and barking of the jackals inhabiting the forests, particularly on full moon nights. That gave me the heebie-jeebies. Enough to keep the blanket pulled over my head, for the entire night. To keep the animals at bay, factory security guards kept a night vigil, banging long bamboo poles on cemented sidewalks as they walked past darkened houses, asleep. This had the desired effect with the jackals fleeing deeper into the green cover of the forests.

The factory siren going off at 6 AM sharp, was like a wake-up alarm. Annoying during holidays, wishing to remain forever under the covers. Baba would be ready in his white cambric cotton pants and white cotton bush shirt, black shoes polished to shine, setting off on foot to the factory, barely a ten-minute walk from our Bungalow. Others who worked in the foundry/steel departments/factory floors, wore Khaki shorts, white colour shirts, and heavy boots. Brown (Indians) and White Sahibs (Englishmen) alike in the same uniform 24/7, 365 days a year.

Ma's clock worked differently. She was up at 4:30 AM, ready to bathe and slip into a freshly laundered saree. Her day always began with the ritual of entering the Puja room, offering prayers, and placing fresh flowers at the feet of the deities. The flowers came from our garden, tended by a grizzled old '*mali*,'(gardener) who ensured we had an uninterrupted supply year-round. Red hibiscus buds, jasmine, and lilies in spring; sunflowers and dahlias in summer; chrysanthemums in winter—along with wild rosebuds.

As a child, I remember the gardener occasionally crafting a bouquet, which Ma would place in a bronze vase on our wooden dining table. These bouquets were rare, reserved for times when the garden yielded a surplus of flowers beyond what Ma needed for her daily puja.

If an especially beautiful rose bloomed, it was cut carefully with its long stem intact and wrapped in silver cigarette foil. Ma would give it to us to take to school as a gift for the class teacher or the nun leading the morning assembly. Carrying a flower to school felt special—each girl proudly presenting a bloom to her teacher was the only acceptable way to show appreciation.

The finest flowers often came from friends with larger, well-tended gardens, where skilled gardeners and enthusiastic parents nurtured the plants with care. Occasionally, some of these elegant hybrid roses, with their long stems and flawless petals, would make their way into the vases of the school chapel, adding a touch of splendour to the sacred space.

To say I was the wild one out of the four would be an understatement. The non-conformist in me surfaced very early on. I never tired of climbing trees, sitting on the guava tree branches, gorging on the half-ripe fruits, rescuing kittens from overflowing drains, cycling around the golf course, swimming and dancing in the rain. Activities one would tend to associate with boys. Indulging in these activities gave me a high, like no other, despite the occasional mishaps, sometimes returning home with cuts and bruises and once a sprained ankle. The latter memory still brings on chuckles and many more acts of dare-devilry, often landing me in serious trouble.

When I was about ten or eleven, I found myself clutching a squash racquet, sitting impatiently in the upper gallery of the court. My sibling and our best buddy were monopolizing the game, deaf to my relentless pleas for a turn. Frustrated, I finally resorted to threats. “I’ll jump down and physically drag you two out!” I declared, pointing to the six-foot drop beneath me.

They burst out laughing, waving off my threat as an empty bluff. "Alright then, here I come!" I announced with dramatic flair before leaping off the gallery like a tragic superhero. Predictably, I landed flat on my skinny, bony backside, twisted ankle and all. Tears of pain and humiliation stung my eyes as I sat there, my busted pride compounded by the unmistakable warmth of pee spreading beneath me.

The scene was absurd: me, sprawled on the court floor, ankle throbbing, dignity in tatters and wet underwear adding to the shame. To their credit, the two culprits did feel a little bad. They hoisted me up and hobbled me home. Thereafter, I was sentenced to two weeks of house arrest with a plastered leg. My heroic leap had cost me not only a turn at squash but also a chunk of my pride.

The '*Jamun*' (Java plum) season brings back more laughs—and another painfully ridiculous memory. The broad trunk of the *Jamun* tree in the backyard was too tall for us kids to climb, so we enlisted the gardener to shimmy up and shake the branches. The purple fruit rained down like magical stardust, scattering across the ground.

In a frenzy, I dashed across the open drain, gathering the fleshy fruits in my frock, which I'd rolled up to create a makeshift pouch. In my excitement, I missed a step and went flying face-first into the drain. The *Jamuns* soared into the air in protest, pelting down on me like purple confetti as I lay sprawled, filthy, and bruised.

My loyal partners-in-crime stared down at me, their goofy grins quickly morphing into full-blown laughter. Their hilarity was so contagious that even I couldn't help but laugh at my misadventure. Covered in muck and *Jamun* juice, I climbed out of the drain, purple-tongued and scratched up, determined not to let Ma discover my mishap.

With my frock a casualty of war, I sneaked past her, heading straight for a long, scrubbing shower to erase all evidence of the day's follies. No way was I going to cry or complain. If there's one thing childhood taught me, it's that a little dignity can survive even the most spectacular disasters.

Growing up with pets

During this period, the animal world entered our home, each one leaving under different circumstances. Out of the many, the first that appears in my mind is a monkey, kept in the garden shed, brought out occasionally to be fed, and patted. The gardener spotted the baby wandering around amongst the flower beds, looking lost and forlorn, in search of his mother, who probably had been chased back into the nearby Sal forests. Baba decided to parent this little guy till he was of age and able to fend for himself. Honestly, I never liked this furry creature, with large round eyes, vying for Baba's attention. Six months later, he was seen bounding off with confidence, probably in search of a mate.

A parakeet with an orange beak, vibrant green feathers, and a long-spotted tail was the next addition to our home. This feisty little bird quickly made its presence felt, taking liberties whenever it was let out of its cage. It would hop onto the dining table and help itself to the food, unbothered by anyone's protests. Though it was most attached to Baba, it also formed a special bond with *Didi*, the eldest sister. The bird would happily perch on her shoulder, observing the household with a sense of ownership.

Despite our many attempts to teach it to sing catchy tunes, the parakeet refused to comply, displaying an attitude far too big for its tiny frame. The only sound it ever uttered from its hooked beak was "*khuku...khuku*," Didi's pet name.

One day, the bird decided it was time to spread its wings—literally—and see the world beyond the confines of its cosy cage. The catalyst? A heated argument between Baba and Didi, during which Didi earned herself a thorough scolding for talking back. When she started crying, *Laljhuti*, the parakeet, seemed to lose its tiny green mind.

Squawking like an avian alarm, *Laljhuti* transformed into a miniature cyclone, zipping through the room at breakneck speed. It knocked over cups and sent saucers crashing, turning perfectly folded papers into a confetti of chaos. In its final act of rebellion, *Laljhuti* delivered precise nips to both Baba and Didi, leaving behind small but meaningful bite marks—souvenirs of its outrage. And then, with a dramatic flair, worthy of a Bollywood hero storming out after a family quarrel, *Laljhuti* shot straight out of the house.

Didi was inconsolable. Her beloved *Laljhuti* was gone. For days, she stood on the veranda, calling its name with the kind of desperation usually reserved for lost lottery tickets. But the green tornado had no intention of returning. *Laljhuti* had flown the coop, leaving behind only chaos, confusion, and a few well-placed dents in family egos.

To console her, Baba brought home a flock of colourful Budgerigars. These cheerful, social birds were more manageable and quickly became part of our household. They lived in a specially built cage, which Baba cleaned daily, ensuring their water and food bowls were always replenished. Their lively chatter often blended with our own, filling the house with a delightful din.

Over time, however, we lost a few of them and Baba decided to set the remaining ones free. With that, the "bird phase" of our lives came to an end, leaving behind memories of fluttering wings and chirping voices.

Next came a bunny rabbit, a fluffball with the whitest fur, pink glassy eyes, and a bushy tail that wiggled with mischief. This little creature was treated like royalty, roaming freely around the house and being pampered with baby carrots.

While everyone adored it, I had my grievances—specifically its habit of leaving tiny black droppings in the most inconvenient places. The worst was finding them nestled in my school shoes. There's nothing quite like starting your day by gagging over rabbit poop.

To this day, I can't recall what became of the bunny. One day it was there, twitching its nose and ruling the household, and the next, its cage had been unceremoniously relegated to the garden shed. Perhaps it hopped off to greener pastures, or maybe someone had finally had enough of the shoe sabotage. Either way, the bunny left its mark—quite literally—all over my childhood memories.

The last one was a surprise birthday gift for me and my twin, which arrived packaged in a shoe box, lined with layers of cotton. A two-week-old Siamese kitten got from a litter of eight and was as tiny as the palm of my hand. I watched Baba and Ma taking turns feeding this one with milk, prying open its mouth and squeezing the cotton ball soaked in milk. He was named "*Tuuta*" and as he grew, the colour of his coat changed from white to grey and then a darker shade of grey. From milk, he graduated to eating goat entrails mashed with cooked rice and was a happy camper, rubbing his back against Ma's legs, perhaps as a reminder it was feeding time. My twin and I fought over him, as one would fight over toys, setting dates for *Tuuta*'s sleeping schedule under our blankets. One week in my bed, the next week in my twin's bed. Soon enough the fights ceased, with "*Tuuta*", going out for overnight dates with the stray cats in the neighbourhood, probably the most sought-after male in the cat kingdom. Reasons could be his debonair looks, his pedigree and the fact that he lived in a Bungalow, served gourmet meals, slept on whichever bed he fancied and most importantly, had his toilet created out of a wooden crate, filled with sand, where he performed his daily business. Cleaned periodically. And if we so much as watched him at his job, he gave the stinky eye as if to say "Get lost. Let me poop in peace"!

His entry/exit route for the overnight dates was through the open bathroom exhaust window. One morning when Ma found he had not turned up for his breakfast, we looked everywhere and found him in the half-filled bathtub with water up to his neck, trying to scramble out, with little success. The philanderer had missed his step on the ledge of the bathtub and landed inside. Of course, that didn't change our love for him. He continued with such escapades, sowing quite a few wild oats, and ended up catching rabies. A very sad end for him and us. My twin and I had to take the rabies injection for a fortnight. Very painful shots in the hips, administered by the Company doctor in the hospital. Thus ended the saga of "*Tuuta*" the Siamese cat with whiskers that tickled, my favourite.

Throwback to when I was an infant—our household included a dog, as I was told, who was, without a doubt, a legend. *Kalu*, a black Indie dog who was often hailed by Baba as the smartest dog in all of Dum Dum, took his babysitting duties very seriously. Whenever my twin and I were left outside lying on mats, sunbathing, *Kalu* was always on guard, keeping a watchful eye over us. He was so dedicated to his job as security guard, that he once caught a thief who had snuck into our first-floor bedroom, carrying off a huge bounty.

According to my *Kaku* (Uncle), *Kalu* didn't just bark at the thief—oh no. He leapt on him, yanked at his lungi, and bit him on the back side, leaving a trail of blood down the steps while barking furiously to alert the family. The thief was eventually caught and locked up for questioning. Sadly, the loot was never recovered, passing through many hands like some sort of criminal hot potato.

Years later, when I moved to Calcutta, *Kaku* shared another hilarious tale about *Kalu* that had me in stitches. Despite his bravery and being fearless about thunder and lightning, unlike the rest of the canine kingdom, *Kalu* had one peculiar, utterly absurd fear: human farts. That's right, a dog who could take on burglars was terrified of a simple "pfft." The moment he heard it, he'd bolt under the bed, tail between his legs. It was impossible to believe that this fearless watchdog was reduced to a quivering mess by such a natural sound.

But the fart-related hilarity didn't end there. Baba had his own stories about the 'natural sound,' often sharing them during dinner, usually with an amused glint in his eye. One of his favourite tales was about his English boss, a man who prided himself on his impeccable manners and love for Earl Grey tea. One day, Baba's boss, while trying to reprimand a worker, lost his composure and let out an enormous "PFT!" that echoed through the room. The poor worker froze, trying not to laugh, while everyone else struggled to maintain their professionalism. Of course, the tale spread like wildfire through the office and quickly became a legend in the staff canteen.

Baba's most memorable story took place at the Club Bar, where his British boss challenged him to a farting competition over mugs of beer and fried peanuts. It was, quite literally, a battle of the gases. Baba and the '*Gora Saab*' (white gentleman) went toe-to-toe, and—surprise—the boss won decisively. He grinned like a champion while the ladies erupted in laughter. Baba, with a straight face, calmly declared, "I let one rip that could have registered on the Richter scale!" We erupted with laughter merely imagining the British boss with Baba turning the place into a comedy club. Was it all true? Or just Baba's storytelling in its finest form? We'll never know for sure. But every time he told the tale, it left us in stitches, imagining a room full of tipsy men and ladies roaring as Baba and his British boss turned flatulence into folklore.

At home, we weren't spared from Baba's musical notes. If we giggled or frowned whenever he let one slip, he'd turn to us, deadly serious, and say, "It's not healthy to hold up the gas building inside!"

Laughter was the secret ingredient to every good day in our household, and Baba was the master chef, dishing out hilarity with a generous side of wisdom. Who would've guessed that something as simple as a fart could ignite profound debates about etiquette and family dynamics? The absurdity of it all only added flavour to life—like a pinch of salt in a sweet dish. It was this unique blend of humour and insight that made our days richer and our bond stronger.

CHAPTER TWO

School...Whispers of Childhood

In sun-drenched fields where laughter soared
We chased the clouds, our spirits roared
With dandelion wishes on the breeze
Barefoot raced, through the tall trees

With pockets of treasures—marbles and stones
The laughter of friends was the heart of our homes
In a world full of wonder, where time stood still,
we painted our joy with the colours of will

Now those days linger like a sweet, fading song
In the tapestry woven, where memories belong
Though the years march on and we wander apart
Childhood's whispers will never part

In the era of branded clothes, no cloth can match the happiness of wearing a school uniform...(unknown) says it all.

I have the fondest memories of my school years which spanned twelve years from 1956 to 1968. All the children living in and around the industrial townships spread over the two states of Bihar and West Bengal attended Loreto Convent, located in Asansol, at that time an important Railway hub of the Eastern Railways. Railway colonies dotted the landscape, homes for railway employees. Due to its strategic location and once home for Britishers, English medium schools mushroomed in the area, run by the Irish Nuns and Fathers—*Loreto Convent* for girls and *St. Patrick's/St. Vincent's* for the boys.

The commute to school was a wild ride, taking a good forty-five minutes to an hour on the Grand Trunk Road, despite it being only 22 kilometres away. On those rare occasions when we arrived late—thanks to a flat tyre or some other misadventure—our excuse of crossing state lines often got us a pass from the Nuns. Sure, they rolled their eyes and let out an exasperated sigh, but hey, we had a solid trump card in our back pocket! After all, nothing says "I'm late because of a flat tyre" quite like a lengthy interstate trek.

The company-provided Blue School Bus is firmly etched in my memory, especially the sight of the old, balding driver at the wheel. His assistant, Usman, was the enforcer of order, ensuring we were all kept in 'straight jackets' throughout the ride, reprimanding us for any hint of mischief.

Our reporting time at the garage was a strict 7:15 AM, which meant dragging myself out of bed at an ungodly hour—every day, without fail, through the oppressive heat of summer, the crisp chill of autumn, and the bone-chilling cold of winter. The winter mornings were particularly brutal, with temperatures dropping to levels that should not be legal. At 6:30 AM, I'd drag myself into the shower, get dressed, wolf down a half-finished breakfast (if I was lucky) and then walk to the garage along with others, often accompanied by a group of 'Ayahs' (governesses), trudging along carrying the heavy school bags and meal baskets.

The door of the Blue Bus stood open, its windows gleaming after a thorough wipe-down and the seats freshly dusted. Usman, dressed in his khaki uniform with brass buttons glinting in the sunlight, stood by the door, ready to assist us as we boarded. The bus was as simple as it was functional—no seatbelts, just two long cushioned benches running along either side, facing each other. There was plenty of room beneath the seats to store our school bags, lunch boxes, and water bottles. The boys boarded first, followed by the girls. Oh! The gender division back then, as if there was an unwritten rule: "Thou shall not talk to boys", extending even to siblings travelling on the same bus. Sisters and Brothers in silence-incommunicado. The senior girls had the honour of sitting near the door and the scramble for the window seats was settled with the kind of diplomacy usually reserved for international peace treaties.

The Blue Bus was our home away from home during school hours, parked neatly in a vacant plot along with other company buses lined up like soldiers in formation. It even doubled as our dining room during lunch break, with Usman pulling out lunch bags from beneath the benches and laying them out on the seats like a maître d' preparing a banquet.

I can't remember the driver's name, but his image is burned into my brain. He was a stout man with salt-and-pepper hair and a face full of overnight stubble that resembled a porcupine's coat. Despite his gruff appearance, he had the kindest eyes and when he wasn't driving, you'd find him napping in the driver's seat, his eyes closed, pretending the chaos around him didn't exist. The only time he spoke was when our voices reached decibel levels that threatened to send the bus into orbit. Then and only then, he'd grumble, "Shush, kids, I'm trying to drive!"

In the end, the Blue Bus wasn't just a means of transportation—it was a little microcosm of childhood: full of rules, routine, and the occasional burst of hilarity, all overseen by a driver who silently tolerated us, his little band of 'unruly' passengers.

I still vividly remember my first teacher in kindergarten. Tall and fair, with permed brown hair that bounced with every step. She wore figure-hugging skirts that added an air of elegance to our little classroom. The click-clack of her stiletto heels echoed down the hall, heralding her arrival and making even the most restless children sit a little taller. With a magical touch, she wiped away tears and enveloped distressed faces in warm hugs, soothing the little ones pulled from their mothers' arms.

Having my twin by my side made the transition smoother; we were like a pair of little ducks waddling into the school routine. Our older sisters were always nearby at break time, a comforting safety net in a sea of new experiences. By the time they were sent off to boarding school in Calcutta, I had settled into the rhythm of school life, feeling less like a fish out of water.

Years later, after I got married, my husband mentioned, a lady secretary at his factory who had once taught at Loreto Convent Asansol. Her first name struck a chord. When we met at an office party, it felt like a scene from a movie. There she was, the kindergarten teacher, with a new surname—still radiant, just as I remembered. Astonishingly, she hadn't forgotten the twins!

Every teacher I had, left their mark, each shaping me in unique ways. Some were strict yet kind, doling out praise for good grades while keeping a watchful eye on the stragglers. The worst punishment was standing against the wall like a mannequin, finger on lips—an unforgettable sentence for talking in class. Somehow, I often managed to slip through the cracks, the goody-two-shoes of the bunch.

Then there was Mother W, the elocution teacher with a ruler that seemed to have a radar for mischief. Her stern demeanour was intimidating, but thanks to her relentless focus on vowels, diction, and grammar, my grasp of English flourished. And how could I forget Mother M? Matronly and nurturing, she ignited my passion for Shakespeare and poetry. "The Merchant of Venice" became my first adventure into the Bard's world, Portia's famous speech etched into my mind as we fumbled through it in class.

Sister S in IX and X made Geography and History as captivating as a storybook, turning history into engaging narratives rather than a series of dates to memorize. Looking back, education was a blend of rote learning with little room for creativity. And Math? Let's just say it was an annual wrestling match with numbers, one I barely managed to escape with passing marks.

Those memories remain vibrant, each teacher a thread in the tapestry of my childhood. Together, they wove a rich fabric of laughter, learning, and nostalgia, bringing a smile to my face even now.

The most memorable year was my last in school, 1968, with Mother JB as our class teacher. Even well into her seventies, she commanded the respect and affection of our entire class—not so much for her teaching skills, but for her delightful sense of humour and charming eccentricities. There were countless moments when she would doze off, mouth agape, while we stifled our laughter. Despite her forgetfulness, her heart was made of gold, and her warmth made that year truly special.

From an early age, I was the one who couldn't resist raising my hand, always eager to answer questions and determined to sit in the front row. However, seating arrangements were based on height, so I usually found myself stuck somewhere in the middle.

Perhaps it was my way of standing out among the forty-five girls in my class, or maybe it was a quiet challenge I set for myself. Was I seeking recognition from my teachers, or was I simply driven by a competitive streak, always striving to do my best?

By eighth grade, the class had thinned out. Some girls left to get married, others took jobs due to financial pressures, and a few moved far away in search of new opportunities. Looking back, I'd rate my efforts as somewhere around a seven or eight. I wasn't at the top of the class, but I was consistent and worked hard, often landing between first and fifth place throughout my school years. What truly motivated me, though, were those moments when I stood on stage at the year-end award ceremonies. The pride of being recognized for my hard work, however big or small, still stands out as a cherished memory. Those experiences taught me that perseverance pays off—whether in big achievements or small victories—and that every step we take shapes who we become.

The education I received from nuns and teachers profoundly shaped my character. I learned the values of punctuality, discipline, compassion, kindness, and integrity. Classes in Moral Science and Gospel Studies enriched my understanding, planting seeds of goodness that would grow within me. Despite being born into a conservative Hindu Brahmin family, I found solace in the teachings of the Bible. Loreto School offered a unique environment where beliefs could coexist. The chapel's doors were always open to all, and I often visited during recess to pray for my family and friends, especially as exams approached. It became a sanctuary where I could unburden my childhood worries.

At one point, I even declared my intention to become a nun, envisioning myself in the convent, teaching at my beloved school. This idea took root after a school retreat—a four-day immersion in self-discipline and spirituality, open to both Catholics and non-Catholics. Captivated by the teachings, sixteen-year-old me naively announced my plan to join the convent after graduation.

This lofty aspiration has since become a cherished family joke, yet I occasionally wonder: what would life have been like as a nun? Would I have been a lively, unconventional Maria from *The Sound of Music*? Or perhaps a wise but cantankerous abbess, doling out tough love? Who knows?

The school campus remains vivid in my memory, an awe-inspiring place of sprawling beauty and unmatched facilities. The hockey field, vast and pristine, could easily rival an Olympic venue, (excuse a little bit of exaggeration here) and served as the centrepiece for our annual sports events. No other school, I'm certain, could boast of six basketball courts, two tennis courts, and a playground brimming with jungle gyms and swings. Expansive green lawns stretched across the campus, dotted with serene ponds—though, intriguingly, the girls were never allowed to approach them. The nuns, always a serene presence, would walk these immaculate grounds, rosaries in hand, silently praying for us and those less fortunate.

My connection with the nuns didn't end when I left school. When I applied for admission to Loreto College in Calcutta for my graduate studies, two of my former teachers were there, making the process a breeze. As a past student, I was exempt from interviews, and later, my daughters enjoyed the same privilege at Loreto House, where they flourished. I attribute part of their success to the legacy of that prestigious institution.

Even five decades after graduating from Loreto College, the school anthem still resonates with me. The lasting impact of a sound education continues to shape my life and the lives of those I love.

Changes along the way

Growing up in a cosmopolitan society laid the foundation for my understanding of oneness in our differences. Cultural variations never hindered lasting friendships; instead, they enriched our lives, expanding our appreciation of our diverse identities as Indians. We celebrated festivals together—Durga Puja, Diwali, Christmas, Easter, and Ramzan—embracing the unique traditions each occasion brought, mingling with classmates from various backgrounds—English, Japanese, French, and first-generation Anglo-Indians. Our differences were mainly superficial—skin tones, hair colours, and features. Some were endowed with natural beauty that seemed to radiate, while others appeared like buds just waiting to bloom. Then there was me, tall and thin, resembling a matchstick girl. I would stand next to my sibling and best friend, who were blossoming into young women, and I'd see nothing but my limbs, like a human giraffe trying to fit in with graceful gazelles. I remember looking in the mirror, feeling a mix of concern and disbelief. "Is that really me?", I'd think, trying to convince myself that being a walking set of limbs wasn't that bad. Secretly, I envied them, practising arm exercises and body stretches like a devoted athlete, in the hope of filling up in the right places. I'd stand in front of the mirror, striking poses as if I were auditioning for a role in a beauty pageant.

"Maybe if I just stretch a little more, the growth spurt would activate", I mused.

While I was desperately trying to "fill out," there was a clear refusal to comply, leaving me feeling like the late-blooming cactus in a garden of roses. I couldn't help but chuckle at the situation: here I was, wishing for a little more "curvature," while my friends, fully equipped, would grumble about how quickly their curves had arrived — it was like the universe had handed out different sets of cards, and I got the flat pack. It was a wild reminder that we all have our struggles, even if they look different on the surface. And maybe, just maybe, it was those little mismatches—those hilarious, "grass-is-greener" moments—that made our friendships bloom in the first place. Because who needs a perfect figure when you've got a great sense of humour and friends who understand the irony of it all?

Surprisingly, puberty arrived for me earlier than for my peers—just two months shy of my twelfth birthday. It was at a relative's home in Calcutta, surrounded by my older sisters. So, when I first noticed the unusual, I panicked, thinking I had somehow cut myself. "Was I wrestling with a rogue pair of scissors?" I wondered. Torn between ignoring it and asking the older sisters, I decided to wait. After all, what could I possibly say? "Hey, *Didi*, do you think I'm injured? Because there's a red situation happening here."

But when the menstrual cramps hit with intense force, I doubled over in pain and finally confided in her. "*Didi*, I think I'm dying!" I exclaimed, half-joking through my discomfort. She laughed and reassured me, explaining that it was normal for girls to bleed each month. "Congratulations! You're officially becoming a woman," she said, with a wink. Aha! I was now part of this new world—a world that seemed to involve a lot of secrecy, rituals, and, apparently, a surprising number of pain relievers. With that, I realized that while the journey might come with its challenges, at least I wouldn't be alone on this ride.

Now that I was on the women's brigade team, it only seemed natural to assume I should start acting and dressing like one. Right? So, within a few months, I insisted on wearing a brassiere. Ma gave me a hesitant look, as if silently saying, "You still have time." But I wouldn't let up. I rattled off the names of my classmates who were already wearing bras—if they could, why not me?

Giving in to my demand, one weekend, we headed to a nearby shopping complex. Ma took me to the lingerie section and asked the man behind the counter for the smallest size available. Did I imagine his raised eyebrow? Maybe. But it didn't bother me—I was thrilled to join the exclusive 'bra-wearing' club.

Ma discreetly tucked the packets under her arms, probably because back then, something as private as bra shopping wasn't exactly meant for public display. The next morning, I felt like it was a special occasion. I proudly donned my first bra for school, eager to let everyone know. The best way to draw attention? Constantly tugging the straps back onto my shoulders, of course. "Welcome to womanhood!" my classmates cheered. I strutted through the school like a peahen, wearing my new bra with all the pride in the world. Girls will be girls, just as boys will be boys!

Hormonal changes took place, as they do—like a surprise party thrown by Mother Nature. Along with this hormonal rollercoaster, thoughts of romance surged in my mind, likely due to an overdose of Mills and Boon novels. I found myself daydreaming about a dashing hero on a white stallion, scooping me up from the highway and galloping off to his castle in Scotland. Spoiler alert: my reality was a bit more... suburban.

Before I knew it, I had developed a colossal crush on my next-door neighbour—an impressive six-plus feet tall, with a voice that could charm a squirrel out of a tree. He was a solid 15 years older, completely oblivious to my "crush", treating me like a kid on the block—specifically, the kind of kid who might colour outside the lines. My dreams of marrying him came crashing down when he popped over to our house and presented his wedding card. Heartbreak? More like a romantic comedy gone wrong!

This was just the start of a series of crushes that rolled in and out faster than toilet paper in a public restroom. Between ages 13 and 16, I found myself navigating countless crushes that never quite went beyond shy smiles and awkward shuffles during dances—basically, a lot of heart palpitations and zero outcomes. If there had been a medal for unrequited affection, I would have been a champion!

One of my biggest crushes was on a brown-haired, fair-skinned boy of British and Anglo-Indian parentage who rode the same school bus. He had an effortless charm that made me feel like I was living in a romantic comedy. I could almost hear a soundtrack playing every time he glanced my way. But then, just like that, he and his family emigrated to Australia. I was heartbroken for days. Who would notice my new hairstyle now, the fringe I'd styled after Bollywood actress Sadhana? I remember thinking, *why can't we have just one romantic montage before you leave?* Instead, I was left with his smile and a lot of "what ifs."

Looking back, I can't help but wonder if it was all in my head. Maybe he didn't notice my fringe at all. Perhaps he was just a kind-hearted boy who appreciated hair fashion in general. *Was it me he liked, or was he just being nice?* I often mused, rolling my eyes at my teenage self. It was an emotional rollercoaster, and I was the one left hanging upside down.

To add insult to injury, there were those girls who got married before passing High school. These lucky ones were "betrothed" from birth, as I later discovered! Thanks to a custom called '*bagdatta*', parents made informal commitments to marry off their children when they reached a marriageable age—which, for some, was shockingly young. "*Do they even know how to be an adult yet?*"

I'd wonder. This practice, supposedly meant to consolidate friendships, felt like an upgraded family plan—complete with all the annoying add-ons of tradition. Archaic customs that was a theme of many Bengali movies based on popular classics, leaving a longingness to be the 'young bride' of the hero starring in the movie. The cutest concept at that time. At fifteen, marriage seemed thrilling through my rose-tinted glasses—age differences be darned! Fast forward and now I'm like, "*Uh, no thanks!*"

Sleepovers at my best friend's house turned into hotbeds of gossip, where we'd spill secrets in the dark, giggling like we were plotting a heist. I even dared to have a crush on Prince Charles, imagining myself gliding up the steps of Westminster Abbey in a flowing white gown, while Queen Elizabeth looked on, probably thinking, "*Not another one*!" Turns out, I wasn't alone; many of us shared those fantasies. After publishing an article online about it, confessions came flooding in—like a support group for hopeless romantics!

Admittedly, those woolly-headed dreams were just part of the growing-up process—silly, yes, but also charming in their own right. Who knew that teenage infatuation could turn into a comedic retrospective? It's all part of the grand adventure of growing up, where every crush is a chapter and every heartbreak is just an unexpected twist in the plot.

Hurdling over

Amid a whirlwind of emotional upheaval, I was determined to excel academically, striving to achieve the coveted five-point score in the Senior Cambridge examination. This required maintaining an average of over 75%—a formidable goal that was both a personal ambition and an expectation from my teachers. However, the years 1967 and 1968 were fraught with challenges that severely tested my resolve and distracted me from my studies.

In 1967, Baba was retrenched from his job, a devastating blow that turned our lives upside down. It wasn't just the loss of his position; it also meant losing the home where we had spent twelve formative years. That house wasn't merely a dwelling; it was a repository of cherished memories, echoing with the laughter of childhood and the love of friends, who felt like family. Leaving it felt as though a part of my soul was being torn away.

The summer of 1968 brought further upheaval as we moved to a distant township, leaving behind our community and sense of belonging. The emotional strain of adjusting to an unfamiliar environment compounded my struggles, and it was clear that these disruptions were taking a toll on my focus and academic performance. Yet, I resolved to persevere, channelling my determination into overcoming both personal and educational hurdles.

Baba's new workplace made daily commuting to school impossible. Faced with no other option, Baba approached the school principal to request that my twin and I be allowed to board at the school for the remainder of the year.

The kind-hearted nuns, who had always supported us during our school years, graciously welcomed us as boarders. Despite their warmth, leaving home was an emotional ordeal for all of us. It was our first significant separation from our parents, and the timing—at such a critical juncture in our academic lives—amplified the emotional weight of the situation.

As the summer holidays ended, my twin and I prepared to leave, each with a single black trunk packed with uniforms, toiletries, and books. At the school porch, we were greeted warmly by Mother J, the principal, and Mother A. While my parents completed the necessary paperwork, the reality of the separation began to sink in.

Tearful goodbyes followed, and at just seventeen, my twin and I felt unready to embrace this new chapter.

Being away from our parents during such a pivotal time was both a mental and emotional challenge. The sense of isolation and longing for home weighed heavily on us. Yet, amid the heartache, I found a renewed sense of purpose. The structure of boarding life and the encouragement from the nuns became a source of stability, allowing me to focus on my studies despite the emotional toll. This separation, though painful, ultimately taught me resilience and the strength to persevere against the odds.

Settling into the hostel brought its own challenges and rewards. Our lives quickly transformed, governed by new routines that, in retrospect, shaped us into more mature and responsible individuals. Those six months were a blend of joy and sorrow. I comforted myself that it was just a six-month separation and that we would soon reunite with our parents.

This change impacted both my health and by extension my performance in the exams. Just three months short of appearing for the exams, I caught mumps from a classmate and spent two long weeks in the infirmary, isolated from my twin and the rest of the school. It felt like I was exiled to a parallel universe where time moved slower than molasses. While the nurse diligently cared for me, coaxing me to eat my lukewarm oatmeal, it was my mother's presence that I missed the most. The nurse's morning and evening visits were like lifelines, filled with gentle reminders about the looming December exams.

Those long days in bed, drifting between wakefulness and dreams, were haunted not just by the dull ache of mumps, but also by the spectres of school lore. Rumour had it that the spirits of nuns lingered in the school's cemetery, their ethereal forms wandering the grounds to comfort the living. I often lay there, peeking through the small window that overlooked the gnarled old tree at the entrance of the Assembly Hall, imagining it to be a gathering place for the dearly departed. I half-expected to hear the rustling of ghostly robes, perhaps even the faint echo of Mother M's voice reciting Shylock's impassioned plea for humanity: "Hath not a Jew hands, organs, dimensions, senses, affections, passions? Fed with the same food, hurt with the same weapons... If you prick us, do we not bleed?"

In my feverish imagination, it felt like a scene straight out of a gothic novel, where the line between reality and the supernatural blurred. Would they rise from the grave, float in and offer me sage advice on how to pass my exams? I pictured them holding a pop quiz from beyond, asking questions about Shakespeare while I struggled to stay conscious.

When the exam results were released in March of 1969, I was in for a rude awakening. A score of 17 points, which, while landing me within the first division, was a far cry from the 5 points my teachers and the nuns had anticipated. It felt disheartening, but thankfully, my parents were more than happy with the results. Their support meant everything.

CHAPTER THREE

Flashes of significant events

I learned the power of connection,
where every smile, each helping hand
Sparked a quiet, deeper reflection

In the warmth of neighbours near,
and the strength of their embrace
I found a place to hold so dear—
A steady, comforting space

The bond we shared, a gentle guide,
Shaped the way I see the world outside
And in its light, I've come to know,
where love and unity truly grow

Having never attended a traditional Bengali wedding, I was ecstatic when the first wedding in our family was announced in 1966. After several failed matchmaking attempts for *Didi*, my eldest sister, an unexpected proposal arrived by mail. It was from a long-forgotten acquaintance—a former next-door neighbour from our ancestral town near Calcutta.

Didi had lived there until she was four. The man, ten years older than her, confessed he had dreamed of marrying her ever since he was a fourteen-year-old boy. What had started as a childhood crush had grown into a deep, enduring love that had stood the test of time.

Ma and Baba were overjoyed upon receiving the proposal. It seemed as though the search for a suitable match had been effortlessly resolved. To them, it felt like divine intervention—how else could such a perfect coincidence be explained? And, to top it all off, he was an ideal match in those days: employed in government service and selected from the prestigious West Bengal Civil Service cadre. With a stable job and a secure future, he appeared to be everything one could hope for in a son-in-law.

I was in class IX and bursting with excitement to experience my first Bengali wedding. *Thakurma*, uncles, aunts, cousins, and even distant cousins from Calcutta and beyond arrived several days ahead of the big day. A few vacant bungalows were transformed into makeshift accommodations, which felt like hosting an elaborate family reunion with a wedding thrown in for good measure.

A small army of cooks was hired to prepare an endless feast of meals and sweetmeats, the latter stored in hefty 10 kg *Dalda* tins—a staple brand of vegetable oil back then. Those tins seemed to empty faster than you could say "*Mihidana*!" (a beloved Bengali sweet).

The house buzzed with life, filled with the clatter of bangles and the cheerful chaos of vegetable chopping, fish descaling, and pots bubbling away. Amid it all, I could hear the not-so-subtle whispers of a few mischievous cousins sneaking bites of *mishti* (sweets) before they even made it to the table!

Since the groom was practically a family heirloom, no formalities were observed as per tradition. It was like a family potluck where the only rule was: the more chaos, the better! The atmosphere was electric and laughter echoed through the halls, making it clear that this wedding would be unforgettable—and not just for the reason of the vows being exchanged!

Didi sitting all decked up in a golden yellow brocaded Banarasi sari, gold necklaces of various lengths hanging down her neck, and hands full of bangles reaching to her elbows, looked like a freshly plucked tulip. Her face exuded radiance. The first granddaughter and the first daughter in the clan had changed identity from the boisterous one to a docile maiden, ready to cross over the threshold of maidenhood in a matter of few hours. Hard to recall the sequence of events, but remember *Didi* looking like a heroine from a Bengali movie with the vermillion streak on her parting, cheeks flushed, looking dazzling. The morning after the wedding reception, *Didi* left, throwing a handful of grains, behind her, symbolic of leaving good wishes for her parents. Climbing onto the Jeep, and driving off to her new home, seemed like I had lost my confidante. Ma and Baba looked broken, as though a part of their body had been severed. Thankfully, the gregarious family clan, hung on for a few days, restoring some measure of cheerfulness in the household, with their incessant chattering, planning meals and competing on emptying the tins of sweets specially prepared for the wedding feast.

The next poignant chapter in my life began with the arrival of my nephew on January 1, 1967—a joyous occasion that made Baba and Ma first-time grandparents and me a '*Mashi*' (aunt). I remember how proud I felt when *Didi* visited with her husband and the little one. Holding that tiny bundle in my skinny arms made me feel so grown-up like I was stepping into a world of adult responsibilities.

The second family wedding took place in the summer of 1968, the same year I was preparing for my Senior Cambridge exams. *Mejdi* (second oldest sister) had already chosen her partner and announced her intention to marry him, but my parents strongly opposed the relationship. As expected, this led to the usual family drama, with a good sprinkling of filmy dialogues thrown in, both sides stubbornly standing their ground. A truce was called with the intervention of relatives. As usual, it was a four-day bonhomie with the family gathering at our house and four days of binge eating. In the end, within two years, I gained a new brother-in-law. These two were truly made for each other, united by their shared love of singing and both were incredibly talented singers. Our tribe thus went up by two counts, and by default, Baba and Ma acquired two sons.

Community life

Community life and the vibrant club culture I experienced as a child were deeply intertwined and centred around socializing and celebrating. Whether at home or the Club, there were always events to mark—be it Rabindranath Tagore's birthday or Diwali celebrations with friends. These moments were an essential part of my upbringing and as I look back, they feel like a chapter from a beloved book that's no longer in print—complete, yet irretrievable. Before I turn the page to the next phase of my life, I feel compelled to share this unique slice of my past.

In our small community, two clubs existed—one for the British and Indian officers and another for the local *Babus* (clerical staff), reflecting the class distinctions that existed during the British Raj. The activities at these clubs offered a delightful mix of entertainment, sports, parties, and social gatherings. The British ladies, draped in long skirts and elegant hats, epitomized grace and composure, while our mothers, in their cotton, silk, and chiffon sarees, radiated warmth and beauty. Surprisingly, there was no awkwardness between them. I often saw them sharing hearty laughs, swapping recipes, and enjoying drinks together, oblivious to any cultural divide. Similarly, the British men mingled effortlessly with their Indian colleagues, chatting over frosty mugs of beer. I observed all this from behind the glass partition, separating the Bar from the library, my imagination running wild with stories of camaraderie and mischief.

But for the children, the real excitement came during the festive parties—Christmas, New Year, Diwali (the festival of lights), and Holi (the festival of colours). Those Christmas parties were pure magic! The treats—paper-thin cucumber sandwiches, dainty pastries, and mountains of candy—felt like they'd been plucked straight out of a Victorian novel.

And the highlight? Mr M, a rotund, jolly Britisher, making his appearance dressed as Santa Claus—arriving, believe it or not, on a sledge pulled by reindeer (or at least, that's what our imagination insisted). With a booming "Ho, Ho, Ho!" he called each child by name, most often mispronounced, to receive their gift.

We'd rush home before the 6 p.m. club curfew for children, clutching our loot like miniature treasure hunters, eager to tear into the brightly wrapped packages. The presents were often dolls, cooking sets, board games, or for the boys, miniature trains and ships.

One particularly memorable Christmas, I unwrapped a Scottish doll dressed in a red-and-black checked skirt with a matching beret. She was the picture of elegance—for a while. Over time, she became my nightly companion, enduring countless tea parties and bedtime adventures. By the end of her tenure, she was missing a glass eye and had more bald spots than hair. But to me, she was perfect, even in her battle-worn state.

The Club boasted world-class sports facilities, including tennis, badminton, and squash courts. While I wasn't exactly an athlete, my sporting mishaps became a family legend. One unforgettable badminton practice saw me swinging my racket with all the grace of a newborn giraffe on ice. Not only did I miss the shuttlecock entirely, but my racket went flying across the court, much to the delight of the laughing spectators. Mortified, I retreated from the court and decided to leave my badminton career behind.

Instead, I found solace in the swimming pool. There, I perfected my breaststroke and relished the water's embrace. However, the diving board was my nemesis. Watching the fearless souls leaping off the edge filled me with equal parts admiration and dread. The mere thought of standing on that board sent my heart racing. Content to cheer from the sidelines, I stuck to my swimming lane, where I felt safe and confident.

Come winter, the pool would close, but the echoes of summer splashes and laughter lingered in my mind. Though I may not have been a natural athlete, the joy of being part of a family that embraced my quirks and celebrated my small victories made it all worthwhile. And perhaps that's the real prize: a treasure trove of stories, love, and a life well-lived.

There were lessons in responsibility, too. The Coca-Cola craze, when it first launched in India, taught me a valuable financial lesson. My daily indulgence in chilled bottles during summer breaks led to a steep rise in Baba's credit bill. When he saw the bill, his reaction was priceless. After a stern lecture on fiscal responsibility, he imposed a "no drinks unless approved" rule. The same happened with the imported chocolates, displayed in the Club Store. This was a pitfall for me, leading to another lesson in spending wisely after Baba introduced a strict "no credit" policy.

Tuesdays were special, marked by Hollywood movies in the club's auditorium—our weekly cinematic escape. My friends and I would dress up, determined to look fabulous and perhaps catch the eye of a crush. It wasn't just about the movie but about making an impression. Later, I found myself balancing academic pressure with a desire to look my best—because, as we all know, you can't have it all, though I tried!

The club's annual New Year's Eve Ball and Banquet were always eagerly anticipated. Baba, in his three-piece suit and bow tie, looked more dashing than any Hollywood heartthrob, while Ma, in her finest saree with her hair elegantly twisted, exuded regal charm. We'd stay up late, eager to hear their amusing stories upon return. One year, Baba recounted how he stopped Ma from accidentally forking a large slice of veal, a dish she didn't eat. That story became a family legend, though Ma eventually avoided the ball altogether, preferring to stay home.

Sooner than expected, the management switched from British to Indian hands, and with it, many rules were relaxed. The most exciting was lowering the age for attending the ball. Yippee! My first ball at fifteen plus was the best news at that time. I couldn't believe my luck! To look adult, I wore a saree, paired with an oversized blouse and silver jewellery. No high heels to borrow—since my mother never wore them—I chose two-strapped leather slippers. It wasn't the most glamorous choice for dancing, but I felt proud of my look.

Arriving at the ball was surreal. The hall was adorned with streamers, and a live band played as couples danced on the floor. I sat awkwardly, feeling like a wallflower, until someone asked me for a dance. The evening was filled with laughter, awkwardness, and a sense of teenage excitement that I would cherish forever.

Sadly, that vibrant lifestyle now feels like a distant memory, tucked away in the archives of the past. Friends who recently visited returned deeply shaken by the stark transformation of a town that once pulsed with life, laughter, and a sense of community. It's a place that once held the fondest of memories, now nearly unrecognizable, its spirit and warmth slipping away in the face of decline. The town that once felt like home has all but vanished, leaving behind only echoes of what it once was.

Looking back, I never felt deprived growing up with the cost-cutting imposed from time to time. Baba excelled in two areas that mattered most to me—food and education—ensuring that the family was always well-fed and well-prepared for the future. While my clothes weren't extravagant, they were thoughtfully chosen, and new outfits were a rare but cherished treat reserved for festive occasions, birthdays and those rare occasions when there was a wedding in the family. Dresses were made from a single bale of fabric, for me and my sisters, giving us a sense of unity and belonging. When I leaf through old family albums, I can't help but chuckle at the four sisters dressed alike, resembling the Von Trapp children from *The Sound of Music*, ready to burst into song.

Reflecting on my childhood, I realise that while some families had more material wealth, our home was rich in warmth and love. I didn't have designer clothes, extravagant birthday parties, or endless luxuries, but I always felt valued and cherished. My parents taught me to prioritise experiences, shared laughter, and family connections over material possessions. As I grew older, I understood that true wealth lies not in things, but in meaningful relationships and a sense of belonging. Their values shaped my worldview, instilling in me the belief that love, kindness, and understanding are the foundations of a fulfilling life. I learned to appreciate the small joys—those everyday moments that come together to create happiness. In this understanding, I found strength, resilience, and profound contentment.

CHAPTER FOUR

To The Big Metropolis

She left the quiet of the fields and sky
The stars she knew, the hills high
With a suitcase full of dreams and grace
She stepped into the city's pace
The streets were loud, the lights so bright
She felt so out of place
A small-town girl, not ready to race

With the Senior Cambridge exams wrapped up in December 1968, it was time to unleash the black tin trunks from the depths of the luggage room. Packing my belongings felt like preparing for a dramatic escape from a beloved summer camp, but instead, we were heading home—leaving behind a phase of life that I can confidently declare was THE BEST. No stress, no judgment, just blissful ignorance and carefree days!

As I boarded the train, it felt like the last nail being hammered in the coffin of school days, sealing away the memories buried in the school cemetery. Arriving at Howrah Station, I scanned the crowd until my eyes landed on Baba, towering above everyone, arms outstretched to embrace the two of us. His welcome was like something out of a movie, only without the dramatic soundtrack as we drove out of the railway station—just the usual chaos of crowds, honking cars, and the sprawling Hooghly River flowing lazily beneath Howrah Bridge. For a small-town girl who had never navigated the bustling streets of Calcutta, it was a sensory overload. The throngs of people, the chaotic traffic, and the towering buildings made me feel like I had stepped into a different universe. Transitioning from living in stand-alone homes, and enjoying the spacious school grounds to a cramped apartment was a shock, too. Climbing up the stairs to our new home, I felt like I was entering a tunnel of unfamiliarity, flanked on one side by similar buildings and on the other by a "*khatal*" (open cowshed).

Mornings greeted me with the melodic mooing of cows and the clanking of iron buckets, courtesy of the '*Goalas*' (milkmen) chattering away in their rustic dialect. The less charming accompaniment was the pungent smell of cow dung wafting through my bedroom window, driving me to burrow deeper under my blanket like a mole seeking refuge.

The biggest challenge, however, wasn't the assault on my senses—it was the reality of sharing a single bathroom. Morning routines became a finely tuned game of strategy, a race against time to align nature's call with everyone else's needs. Inside, one person was desperately focused on their task, while outside, another was equally desperate, doing their best to hold it in. The rhythm of our mornings was unmistakable, marked by the urgent *bang, bang, bang* on the bathroom door—the daily anthem of distress.

When Baba finally answered the call of the masses, he would emerge serenely with *The Statesman* tucked under one arm and a Gold Flake cigarette dangling from his lips. His expression was one of calm detachment—like a Tibetan monk fresh from meditation. Except, of course, for the trail of cigarette smoke he left behind, a hazy souvenir for the next hapless occupant.

Baba's bathroom habits were legendary. "Potty time" was his sacred ritual, a retreat that demanded absolute privacy. Newspapers, magazines, and even novels accompanied him, transforming the bathroom into his personal reading nook. Whether contemplating life's mysteries or catching up on cricket scores, he found his peace in that tiny sanctuary, oblivious to the chaos brewing just outside the door.

Ma, on the other hand, was a creature of habit. She adhered to her sunrise schedule, rising even before the birds had finished yawning in their nests. There was never a clash in timing with her—she simply did not need to rush.

Mornings thus became a whirlwind of chaos and clock-watching, ending with a collective vow to find a place with more toilets, because of the current setup. And soon enough, during one of his evening walks, Baba discovered a more spacious apartment—one with not one, but two lavatories and two shower rooms! The daily banging at the bathroom door finally ceased, and Baba could now enjoy his newspaper in peace, with cigarette curls rising to the ceiling like little flags of victory. Watching Amitabh Bachchan playing the character of *'Piku'* (Bollywood movie) and his bathroom antics, reminded me of Baba's habits, though thankfully, he never went as far as carrying a mobile special toilet when travelling. Toilet stories seemed the topic of avid discussion in Bengali households as shown in the movie and personally experienced. The smiles or furrowed brows, plastered on the faces of those emerging from this private sanctuary, were an index for measuring satisfaction levels. Never mind the detailed discussions that followed ranging from colour, texture, and quantity of output vs. input.

During the first six months in the city, with nothing much to do, I became a certified expert in the fine arts of eating, sleeping, reading, and the occasional marathon session of lazing around. All of this was accompanied by the quiet dread of waiting for exam results to be declared. Baba and Ma, ever cautious, had one golden rule: no venturing out alone. Weekends, though, were a different story—Baba turned into our personal tour guide, leading us on mini-explorations of the city we had been born in but barely knew.

Every outing felt like an adventure, whether it was clambering onto a bus, gliding along in a tram, or cruising in one of Kolkata's iconic black-and-yellow taxis. One weekend, we gawked at the majesty of the Victoria Memorial; another, we stuffed ourselves silly at Anadi Cabin, where we discovered the magic of '*Dhakai paratha*' (fried flatbread) and '*kosha mangsho*' (spicy mutton curry). Baba had an uncanny knack for turning every outing into a gastronomic escapade and our taste buds rejoiced at every pit stop.

The fun wasn't just limited to food. Movie outings at Metro Cinema were another highlight. Baba always picked the latest Hollywood or Bollywood blockbuster for us. One such outing was to see *Mera Naam Joker* (yes, the one with the legendary Raj Kapoor). Dinner followed at one of Baba's favourite restaurants, rounding off the evening in culinary and cinematic glory. But even amid all the weekend excitement, the looming shadow of exam results was never far from my mind, threatening to crash the party at any moment.

Back then, staying connected with friends was a Herculean task. No phones at home meant gossiping with school buddies was off the cards. The only way to bridge the communication gap was through trunk calls—a marvel of patience and frustration in equal measure. These calls took an eternity to connect, only to cut off at the most inconvenient moments, leaving everyone hollering "Hello? Can you hear me?", into the void.

By mid-March, my anxiety had reached fever pitch. The exam results were out, and I was a walking bundle of nerves. Baba, on the other hand, was cool as a cucumber. One evening, he returned home grinning like he'd won the lottery. Turns out, the grin wasn't for a jackpot but because my twin and I had both passed! Sure, it was a shaky first division, but while I felt deeply disappointed, Baba and Ma were unfazed. Their parenting philosophy? Education mattered, but they weren't the kind to crack the whip. Grades were never the centrepiece of family discussions. Instead, they focused on making sure we were equipped to handle life with integrity and resilience.

Then came the exciting question: what next? My options boiled down to graduate studies in either Geography or Literature. The hunt for the best colleges began. Lady Brabourne College in Park Circus topped the list, closely followed by Loreto College in Middleton Row. Loreto won out, thanks to its proximity to Baba's office.

The admission process was nothing short of magical. Accompanied by Baba, I arrived at Loreto College, where Sister S greeted us warmly. There were no long queues, no gruelling interviews—it was as if the universe had rolled out the red carpet. A few days of deliberation later, I settled on Geography for my Honours course, with dreams of pursuing a Master's in Geology down the road. And so, my academic journey began—with twists, turns, and of course, the occasional '*Kabiraji cutlet*' (a popular dish originating from Kolkata made of spiced mince, covered in crumbs and batter fried), from Anadi Cabin to fuel my ambitions.

But before I could revel in my newfound independence, there was a significant hurdle to overcome: the fine art of navigating public buses. The ten-minute trek to the bus stop felt more like a pilgrimage, especially when lugging a bag that seemed to contain half the college library. Every journey was a trial, with buses either arriving as sardine cans on wheels or disappearing entirely, leaving me staring down the road with a mix of despair and indignation.

And yet, despite the bumps (literal and metaphorical), life in the city was thrilling—a mix of discovery, anxiety and the excitement of travelling on public transport. Who knew adulthood would taste so good? The first hurdle in my grand adventure of city life was thus, mastering the art of travelling on public buses. Knowing that we were babes in the 'urban' woods, Baba had carefully written down the bus route numbers for us, creating a little treasure map. One option was to get off at Park Street Crossing and walk down the street to reach the imposing front gate. Alternatively, to hop off at the bus stop across from the Standard Chartered Bank on Chowringhee Road, which offered a much shorter walk to the back gate. It took some time to figure out the best routes, much like solving a jigsaw puzzle with the city map, while trying to avoid the overcrowded buses.

Bus travel initially felt like a chaotic adventure in zero gravity. Balancing books and handbags was a circus act in itself, and when all the seats were taken, clinging to the overhead rod while standing, became a survival skill I desperately lacked. Whenever the driver slammed the brakes, I was propelled down the aisle like an out-of-control bowling pin, scattering passengers' laughter in my wake.

But after a few months, I became a seasoned bus warrior. Pushing my way onto the bus felt like competing in a game show. Niceties were abandoned—the only rule was to claim the first vacant seat and ignore anyone boarding after me.

Disembarking was another art. A sharp shout to the conductor was all it took to halt the bus. The conductors, ever the hustlers, seemed to sense new passengers a mile away and expertly held off the other passengers in a hurry to disembark, until I made my (not-so-graceful) exit.

Now while I fully endorse the general agreement that in Calcutta, ladies enjoy a level of respect and privileges that make you feel like royalty, there were incidents not so pleasant, I faced in the mayhem of bus rides. During my three years of navigating this delightful chaos while attending college, I unwittingly enrolled in a masterclass on fending off the occasional 'grabbers,' 'pinchers,' and 'elbow diggers'. No denying that they existed, though few and far between. On those rare occasions, it felt like I was living in a twisted game of dodgeball, where the goal was to avoid unwelcome hands instead of balls. It turned out to be a learning process that went into identifying the potential ones and steering clear of them in crowded buses. And soon I became a pro at wielding my handbag like a medieval knight brandishing a sword, ready to defend my personal space. It wasn't just about survival; it was a full-on performance art! I'd stand there, swaying with the rhythm of the bus, mastering the art of side-eye and quick footwork, while navigating this crowded battlefield. My friends and I would often giggle about our 'bus combat techniques' over cups of chai, bonding over our shared war stories like seasoned veterans. Who knew that amidst the jostling and chaos, we'd become the unwitting queens of the bus—regal in our ability to fend off unwanted attention while still maintaining our dignity (and the occasional laugh)? Ah, the mishaps of public transport are neatly punched and stored in memory files.

Reflecting on those three years of travelling in public buses, I realized it was like taking a maturity pill for a small-town girl blossoming into a city maiden. I learned resilience, resourcefulness, and how to navigate the chaotic currents of urban life—skills that would serve me well for years to come. Each bus ride was an adventure, a life lesson, and I emerged from it all ready to take on whatever this vibrant city had in store for me!

Returning to the present, it's hard to accept that my birth city will soon be saying goodbye to the Tramway service, the oldest operating tram system in India, long synonymous with Calcutta. And as if that loss wasn't enough, the yellow cabs—those iconic symbols of the city—are reportedly being replaced as well. Whatever the reasons behind these changes, they mark the end of an era. A part of the city that I've known and loved for over two decades will soon be swept away, making way for something new. The thought of unlearning the familiar and relearning the city in its new avatar fills me with quiet sorrow. How can you reconcile with a city that no longer feels the same?

There was no room for bunking classes while chasing an honours degree—no way to slip out unnoticed like some secret agent. Those brave souls in the Pass degree, however, had it down to a fine art. They'd stealthily glide out the back gate, meeting up with their boyfriends from St. Xavier's for a cheeky matinee or a stroll along Park Street, the heartbeat of Calcutta, where the vibrant energy never seemed to wane.

When it came to dressing appropriately, Loreto College had an unwritten dress code that felt almost like a badge of honour—a secret handshake of sorts. Hemlines had to fall well below the knee (several inches, to be precise), necklines were required to sit high above any suggestion of cleavage, and strappy dresses were strictly forbidden.

The student body was a vibrant mix of regular students and the children of celebrities, bureaucrats, and industrialists. Any deviation from the code—a fashion faux pas—would result in being promptly sent home to "reassess your wardrobe choices" and return looking like a proper lady. You could practically feel the collective relief of the faculty every time a rebellious hemline was brought in line.

As for eating in the College Canteen? Well, that was reserved for monumental occasions—like a birthday celebration that felt like winning the lottery. My pocket allowance was enough to cover travel expenses, with a margin for ice cream if any savings accrued on days I got a car lift. And, much like school days, Ma packed lunch for college as well. Mostly had out on the green lawns with friends sharing boxes like a happy family picnic. There was something comforting about the familiarity of that routine—like a well-worn pair of shoes. Speaking of shoes, two pairs saw me through the three years. Likewise, regarding wardrobe change, I never felt the need to sport a new outfit every single day, unlike some of my batchmates who treated their wardrobes like a catwalk. I had my few sets that rotated like a trusted playlist, and honestly, no one cared. Sure, I was a bit envious of those with closets bursting with the latest trends, but it was more of a fleeting thought, like wishing I could visit Flury's every day after college for their lip-smacking pastries. Loreto taught me a valuable lesson in humility, helping me shed my self-consciousness. Instead, I found myself focusing on what truly mattered—studies, friendships and those rare moments of carefree laughter.

Then there was Geography, a subject that opened up a world of travel. Our practical course required us to gather data and compile a thesis based on fieldwork. In our third year, we set our sights on a remote village in Rajasthan—Jawai Bandh, to be precise. Armed with theodolites (instruments used for measuring angles both horizontally and vertically) and all the gear that looked straight out of a science fiction movie, fourteen of us, if memory serves me right, along with two professors, boarded the train at Howrah Station, excitement buzzing through the air like electricity.

We had built-in sightseeing days, with a stop in New Delhi coinciding with Diwali, the festival of lights and on the return, a pit stop at Ajmer for those wishing to pay their respects at the revered Khwaja Moin-Ud-Din Chishty Darga. That was my longest train journey yet, and it sparked a travel bug in me that has never quite faded.

In those cramped train compartments, surrounded by friends and laughter, I realized that the adventures we embarked on and the memories we created were worth more than any designer outfit. After all, life is a journey, and I was just getting started.

Career - 1973 onwards

After graduating from college, I found myself adrift again. Should I pursue further studies or jump into professional courses? The thought of relying on Baba for more years weighed heavily on me. He was nearing retirement, and while he would have supported my request, I couldn't shake the feeling of burdening him. With job opportunities for fresh graduates scarce, my options were limited: get enrolled for a B.Ed. from Loreto College to become a teacher or dive into the corporate world as it began opening up for freshly minted graduates. Coming from a middle-class home, there were roadblocks in pursuing other professions. But that did not stop me from indulging in a moment of mischief. With trepidation, I suggested that I might follow in the footsteps of several friends and become an air hostess. His reaction was immediate. "Not everyone is cut out for this profession. Moreso, girls from middle-class backgrounds," he asserted; eyes wide with concern.

"Why not?" I asked, genuinely perplexed.

"You would be a misfit!" he replied as if I'd proposed joining a circus. I rolled my eyes internally but respected the intensity of his gaze.

I knew he wasn't criticizing the profession itself; he was worried about the unpredictability that came with it—travelling to different cities, staying in various hotels and the potential risks of a life on the road. I couldn't deny that the thought of constant travel was thrilling, but deep down, I understood his concerns. The idea of living out of a suitcase and navigating unfamiliar places wasn't something I was ready for just yet. With a silent sigh, I chose to let the conversation drift, grateful for his protective instincts even if I didn't share his fears.

Stepping into the corporate world was an exciting prospect, especially after hearing the success stories of a few who had made it big. Inspired by their journeys, I enrolled in the Pitman's Commercial Course, focusing on shorthand, typing, and bookkeeping. It felt like I was turning a corner, ready to embrace whatever lay ahead. However, I couldn't shake off my concerns about entering a mixed-gender environment. Having spent my entire education in an all-girls school and college, the idea of working alongside men was daunting. I found myself wondering if I would be able to navigate the dynamics of a male-dominated workplace. Would I feel comfortable expressing my ideas? Would I be taken seriously? It was very much a man's world back then, and I questioned whether I had the confidence to hold my own. I worried about potential biases. These thoughts swirled in my mind, mingling with excitement, as I prepared to step into an unfamiliar realm. Ultimately, I knew I needed to face these challenges head-on if I wanted to thrive on my new path.

After I completed my course, the job market sprang to life. In the early seventies, there was a sudden surge in demand for convent-educated graduate stenographers. This demand arose from the emigration of Anglo-Indian secretarial staff to other countries, leaving behind numerous office vacancies. As Indian managers stepped in to replace the departing expatriates, they required secretaries who could effortlessly bridge the gap between the two worlds.

My first unsolicited interview call came before my Pitman's certificate even arrived. The couple running the institute sent me to a social service organisation on Russel Street. The manager, a kind-hearted elderly gentleman, quickly eased my anxieties about this new environment. His secretary, a young woman from Mizoram, was a gem—helping me shed my shyness and scepticism about the "big bad wolves" of the corporate world. Within six months, I was thriving in my work, enjoying the camaraderie, and feeling completely at ease.

When I handed in my resignation to pursue new opportunities, the manager was genuinely sad to see me go but also proud of my progress. It was a bittersweet moment, reflecting how far I had come in such a short time. Little did I know then, that this would be just the beginning of my journey in the corporate world.

I worked for barely two weeks at a recording company in Dalhousie Square, before I chanced upon an ad in *The Statesman* looking for graduate stenographers and quickly submitted my application. I was called for an interview. My brother-in-law, who was more like an older brother to me, kindly offered to accompany me. I was grateful for his support, as getting lost in the city was the last thing I wanted. As we drove in his government vehicle, he encouraged me the whole way, boosting my confidence and lifting my spirits. His reassuring presence made me feel less anxious about the interview and more excited about the opportunity ahead. With every passing moment, I felt my resolve strengthening, ready to embrace whatever came next.

On the day of the interview, I dressed meticulously in a saree, pleats pinned just right, hair braided, and leather slippers that I desperately hoped wouldn't betray me. Clutching my folder of certificates, I stepped into the office on Hare Street, a colonial relic with a rickety old lift that moved up like it would take forever. As I handed my interview letter to the receptionist—an attractive Anglo-Indian woman in a form-fitting dress, hair coiffured, and a pleasant smile—I felt utterly out of place. "Well, this is it," I thought. "Goodbye, dreams!" I tried to discreetly hide the slippers beneath the hem of my saree while other girls in the waiting area exuded confidence. When my name was finally called, I nearly jumped out of my skin. My brother-in-law nudged me forward, whispering, "You got this!"

The office I entered was filled with glass cubicles, and the first person I met was the Branch Secretary. She was like a warm hug in human form, easing my worries.

"Why pursue a corporate job when there are no growth opportunities?" she asked, glancing pointedly at my academic records. Without missing a beat, she added, "With your qualifications, you'd be a much better fit in the banking sector or at one of the leading newspaper houses. Let me put it plainly—the next vacancy for a secretary in this office won't open up for another fifteen years!" Her tone left no doubt that she had no plans of leaving anytime soon.

"*Well, I didn't know that when I signed up*!" I thought but only managed a sheepish smile in response.

After meeting the elderly Branch Manager, I was assigned a consumer complaint to handle independently. With my heart racing, I jotted down his instructions in shorthand and then typed them up on a clunky manual typewriter. I couldn't shake the feeling that others were giving me odd looks, but maybe I was just imagining it.

What convinced me to accept the position, if offered, was the sight of older employees working at their desks, radiating stability and a safe environment. The employment letter arrived within a week, and I reported for work on August 3, 1973, with a desk in the Branch Secretary's room as her understudy.

There were some surprises in store. When the Branch Manager handed me my employment letter, he asked, "What are your salary expectations?" I blinked at him, completely unprepared. "Um... I wasn't sure what to expect?" I stammered. With a warm smile, he shared the salary figure of Rs.650 per month and my jaw nearly hit the floor. Not that I had any clue what the figure meant in terms of purchasing power, but with the add-ons of annual bonuses, reimbursement of medical expenses and lunch coupons...felt like winning the lottery! I signed on the dotted line, my heart racing with excitement. I was the first graduate convent-educated stenographer to join the Branch, and I was ready to dive into this new chapter of my life. Little did I know, this journey would span eighteen years—filled with laughter, challenges, and a few more surprises along the way.

Was I imagining an underlying resistance from my colleagues? I could sense my presence was a juxtaposition to their established routines. Whispers and sideways glances seemed to follow me, raising doubts about whether I could survive in such a working climate. Perhaps my choice of traditional outfits and make-up-less face often drew attention, and I felt like an outsider in a world that celebrated a different aesthetic. I watched the female staff with awe glide through the office in their smart Western attire, perfectly matched handbags swinging at their sides, heels clicking rhythmically on the floor, and faces adorned with expertly applied makeup. They exuded an air of confidence that felt foreign to me, which I lacked by miles.

In those moments, I couldn't help but feel like a misfit, struggling to find my place in an environment, starkly different hitherto. It was as if I were caught between two worlds: one that embraced the familiar comfort of my cultural roots and another that demanded conformity to an unspoken standard. The isolation weighed heavily on me, and I yearned for acceptance, hoping that over time, my colleagues would see beyond my appearance and recognize my dedication and capabilities. In such a scenario, at first, I felt like a stranger in this world. If it hadn't been for the comforting presence of the 'mother figure' in the office and a few senior officers who reminded me of Baba, I might have considered leaving. But I was determined to break the ice and find my place among them.

It didn't take long for the tide to turn. Acceptance began to blossom, largely during our lunch breaks. The act of sharing food became a bridge between us. Those exchanges became the foundation of lasting friendships.

Once my six-month probation period ended, I was thrilled to be confirmed as a permanent employee, and my workstation was moved to the open area next to the clerical staff. In those days, there were three levels of staff, apart from the Branch Manager and Assistant Branch Manager: officers, clerical employees, and subordinates, which included peons, dispatchers, godown keepers, and drivers. Despite this clear class distinction on paper, our interactions during work hours were warm and collaborative, transcending these divisions. Transitioning from a sheltered life to working in a mixed environment was an adjustment process, yet I soon found a sense of comfort in my new work environment. It became a second home; one I grew to cherish over the years.

Most multinational companies of repute in Calcutta, back then, followed the practice of extending special privileges to the female staff, providing home pick up and drop. This was a huge plus point for the ladies, in not having to spend time on public transport, reflecting the City's cultural ethos that honoured and safeguarded women in the workplace. This respect for women was a cornerstone of my experience, and it shaped my eighteen years with the company into a journey of camaraderie, growth, and mutual respect. As I look back, I realize that the connections I formed and the environment I thrived in were invaluable, transforming my initial apprehension into a profound sense of belonging.

Earning a salary, gave me a sense of independence and enabling power. Having minimal personal requirements to spend on myself, I felt great pride in handing over my monthly salary envelope to Baba with the satisfaction of contributing to running the household expenses. My only expense was in buying books and upgrading my wardrobe. As and when I felt the need to upgrade my wardrobe, Baba gladly went out shopping with me for sarees. That was the only attire I wore for work, right through those eighteen years. Wearing make-up seemed alien. Watching my colleagues redoing their makeup after lunch break, interested me somewhat. Slowly I picked up the rudiments. Never perfecting it. Rather ending up looking like a mess. And to add insult to injury, one day Baba and Ma, told me up to my face "Cut it out. It doesn't suit you". Thus, came to an end to any further attempts to look suave and sophisticated. My make-up kit had only a kajal eye pencil, and a puff to powder my sweaty face with talcum powder...favourite brand '*Cuticura*'. I got interested in make-up, just before marriage. After all, how can a bride look like she was attending a funeral? So, my colleagues became my makeup advisors, teaching me the steps in applying all the magical lotions to look like the front-page face in Vogue magazine. And that brings me to a hilarious situation that happened the first time I went out shopping with my beau just days before our marriage.

I was in a spendthrift mood, enjoying randomly picking up the costlier brands of makeup for use on my wedding day. He stood patiently watching and mentally calculating the amount I had spent on makeup alone, assuming this would be a monthly billing, in the future. Later he confessed to being alarmed at how expensive it would be to maintain a wife of my standards, least aware; that it was a one-off spending! We still laugh over it, more now that the need for any make-up has been replaced with the need to wear face masks at all times, with Covid tail lights still visible in the distance.

Office politics and gossip were common in every organization, and ours was no exception. However, thankfully, nothing ever escalated into serious conflict or reputational harm. I never encountered sexual harassment; instead, the work culture was refreshingly professional and supportive, fostering an environment that felt both collegial and familial. It was as close to a home-like atmosphere as one could find in a workplace.

The company's commitment to its people was evident in times of both joy and sorrow. When tragedy struck, such as the untimely passing of a colleague, the company went above and beyond, offering employment opportunities to their children—a remarkable policy that ensured continuity and care.

I experienced this care firsthand in 1986 when I was diagnosed with ischemic heart disease at just 34. The support I received from my superiors and colleagues was overwhelming. They showed genuine concern, granting me time off to recover. Colleagues visited and checked on me, their kindness deeply touching.

Though my life felt as though it had crumbled, I refused to succumb to despair. My determination to overcome this challenge was driven by my responsibilities as a daughter, wife, and mother to my young girls. The company doctor played an essential role in my recovery, conducting a series of tests that ultimately revealed a misdiagnosis through an echocardiogram, a diagnostic tool still relatively new at the time.

When I returned to work, I refused to let my health issues define me. I joked with colleagues that my heart was merely a dramatic diva seeking attention! Each shared laugh reinforced the strength of our supportive community. Despite facing significant challenges, the warmth and kindness of those around me made all the difference, reminding me that resilience is not just about overcoming obstacles, but about the people who have your back, along the way.

This spirit of care and compassion was the backbone of the organization. Employees rarely left for better opportunities; most stayed until retirement. In my eighteen years of service at the Calcutta Branch of Nestle India Limited, I can count on my fingers the resignations that came in. I envisioned myself retiring gracefully at the age of 60. But, as life often does, fate had other plans...

1987 was a life-turning point. Consequent to the Branch Secretary's retirement in December 1986, a vacancy arose to fill the position. The Branch Manager had already recommended me for filling the position. Meanwhile, there was resistance to contend with from staff who felt, the position should rightly have gone to a senior colleague, as was the system prevailing back then. The promotion letter confirming my new position, as Branch Secretary as of 1st January 1987, came with mixed feelings. Was it fair? Would I be able to handle the task ahead, in a changing environment? The advent of technology taking over manual systems was already slipping in with the introduction of the payroll as a start. A huge change. A change that meant, unlearning and relearning systems and practices. Without a formal handover/training, I felt like being thrown into the rough seas without a life jacket. I had to stay afloat or die. Survival meant changing my mindset and focusing on learning new ways. From mainframe to desktop, the change entailed a massive amount of data entry, ensuring no mistakes. The

IT department from Head Office visited a couple of times to initiate me into the processes involved.

That year marked a significant transition, with the old giving way to the new. A fresh, young Branch Manager stepped into the shoes of his predecessor, who had retired that same year. Change, as we all know, rarely comes without its fair share of dissent, acceptance, and the challenge of adapting to modern management principles. It's a delicate exercise in shifting mindsets, and we all felt the weight of this transformation. After years of stability under the former manager's leadership, many were hesitant to embrace this new approach. Some clung to the familiar routines and practices, wary of the changes that lay ahead. It's a natural response—comfort and familiarity often create a cocoon that's hard to break. Naturally, in the face of change, the willingness to adapt felt like an uphill battle.

The new Branch Manager brought a refreshing perspective. He was not only competent and energetic but also possessed a unique kindness that made him approachable. His philosophy of "knowing the way, going the way, and showing the way" (a nod to John Maxwell) resonated deeply. He understood that leading a team through change requires more than just directives; it calls for empathy and understanding.

Under his guidance, we began to navigate the waters of transformation together. He organized workshops and team-building exercises that encouraged open dialogue, allowing to voice concerns and fears. Gradually, the initial resistance that once seemed insurmountable started to dissolve as the realization dawned that adaptation didn't mean losing one's identity; instead, it meant growing and evolving together.

As new strategies began to take root and show results, a shift occurred. Everyone started to see the benefits of modern management principles, and the fear of change morphed into curiosity and, eventually, acceptance. The journey wasn't without its bumps—at times, it felt like working at cross purposes, reluctant to let go of old practices while learning to embrace the new. And with each small victory, the team began to unite, driven by a shared goal of not only adapting but thriving in this new environment. The combination of our new manager's supportive leadership and the collective willingness to adapt ultimately forged a stronger, more resilient team.

Change, while uncomfortable, can also be a catalyst for growth is what we experienced as we moved forward. It taught us to blend the wisdom of experience with the fresh ideas of youth, creating a dynamic environment where everyone's voice mattered. With his IIM background, the training of sales staff had the desired facelift, showing fresher and newer ways of running a company. These helped unzip the archaic ways and replaced them with modernistic approaches. Without a doubt, my learning curve went up during his tenure as Branch Manager. With his transfer, the position was filled by yet another young IIM graduate. I had the privilege of working with him for two years. A 'no fuss person', devoid of the 'boss syndrome', more a friend than a boss. His dynamic personality and easy-going nature were his USP. Proud to have known and worked for both of these dynamic leaders, who went on to become hugely successful in their respective careers.

Insights

In today's fast-paced, interconnected world, leadership styles profoundly shape organizational culture. My experience working under younger, professionally qualified bosses offered invaluable lessons that significantly influenced my professional outlook and personal growth. These leaders demonstrated the importance of innovation, adaptability, empathy, and a clear vision—qualities essential for navigating the complexities of large organizations.

One of the most striking attributes of my young bosses was their unwavering commitment to innovation. They were unafraid to challenge the status quo, encouraging the team to think beyond conventional boundaries. Their mantra—"There are no bad ideas; every thought has the potential to spark something great"—created an environment where creativity thrives. This mindset liberated the team from the fear of judgment and fostered a culture of experimentation. From this, I learned that true leadership involves taking risks and inspiring others to do the same, empowering them to explore new possibilities without hesitation.

Another defining quality was their adaptability. In the face of changing market dynamics, they exhibited a remarkable ability to pivot strategies when initial plans failed to deliver results. Rather than clinging to ineffective approaches, they called for reassessment, encouraging the team to gather fresh insights and develop alternative solutions. This taught me that effective leadership is not about rigidly sticking to a plan but about being flexible and responsive. In a world where change is constant, the ability to adapt is essential for success. Great leaders recognize when to shift gears and motivate their teams to view change as an opportunity for growth.

Perhaps the most profound lesson I learned was the value of empathy in leadership. These young bosses were approachable, taking a genuine interest in the well-being of their team members. They made it a priority to check in regularly—not just about work but also about personal matters. This emphasis on emotional well-being fostered trust and collaboration within the team.

As I observed their leadership, I realized that connecting with people is at the heart of effective leadership. Empathy creates a supportive work environment where individuals feel valued, understood, and motivated to contribute their best. A leader's ability to listen and respond to their team's needs can enhance morale and drive productivity.

Through their example, I learned that great leadership is a blend of innovation, adaptability, and empathy, all underpinned by a clear vision. These qualities not only strengthen teams but also equip leaders to inspire growth and resilience in an ever-evolving professional landscape.

CHAPTER FIVE

Shifting Horizon

In the quiet dawn of a single day
She danced with dreams, in her ballet
A hand to hold, a heart to share
Her world expands with love and care
From "I" to "we," the shift begins
New chapters are written, where life spins
In shared mornings, laughter and tears
She learns the depth of love through the years

1975-Shifting Horizons

For every woman—or shall I say, most women—marriage is like taking a blind curve on the road. You think you know what's ahead, but whoosh! Surprise! Within two years of starting my career, I hopped onto the married bandwagon and acquired a shiny new surname. A marriage without a script, mind you. While my father, Baba, was busy scouting suitors within the esteemed Bengali Brahmin community, the rebel in me had other plans.

Sundays became my secret mission. Unbeknownst to Baba, I would eagerly dive into the matrimonial column, armed with a cup of chai and a sense of adventure. And then, presto! There it was "***Wanted tall and pretty match of any caste and province for a Hindu bachelor (27), Engineer M.S. from Canada from a very respectable and well-placed family of UP., tall (179 cms.), handsome, working in a British firm in Calcutta in management cadre. Write in detail to Box 2509, Statesman, Calcutta),*** published on June 15 1975, in the matrimonial supplement (quoted 'as is' from the newspaper cutting stored away, a cherished memento of a time when dreams felt just within reach). This was just up my alley!

Without consulting Baba, I crafted a response, borrowing generously from his previous letters to prospective grooms for my older siblings, somewhat exaggerated—who doesn't? Parents never see flaws in their offspring anyway. I slipped the letter into the mail via the office peon, feeling quite like a covert operative.

Returning home one evening, Baba waved a letter in front of me—one he had received in response to my response. His eyebrows furrowed as he read the details from the groom's father, who signed off with a name that didn't exactly scream "Bengali Brahmin." He shot me a suspicious glance. "Did you have any hand in this?"

With my heart racing, I blurted out the truth. We discussed the pros and cons of an inter-state marriage at length. Cultural differences, food habits, and other roadblocks were laid bare as if Baba held a magnifying glass over every potential pitfall. But I knew what I wanted and managed to convince him, setting a date for our first meeting.

And so, in walked my potential husband—a tall, handsome guy with a moustache that could rival Tom Selleck's and sideburns that were all the rage. Dressed in a rust-coloured short-sleeved shirt and brown pants, he looked like he had just stepped out of a 1970s catalogue. In a casual setup, we chatted over cups of tea and snacks in Baba's presence. The meeting ended with no commitments from either side.

Baba's reaction was favourable right from day one. He was all on board—except for one tiny detail: I had never set foot in a kitchen. "How will she fit into a strictly vegetarian household?" he wondered aloud, probably envisioning me running amok, tossing non-veg dishes like confetti. To be honest, the kitchen was off-bounds for us girls. So, no one was to blame that I had never even made myself a cup of tea, let alone the thought of cooking a vegetarian or non-vegetarian meal.

We dated for six months, which in those days meant cosying up in the living room with someone or the other in the family hovering nearby and making an appearance on the pretext of bringing tea and snacks. Except for one daring escapade? A trip to Diamond Harbour, with Baba's permission. Travelling in a local train, I felt like a fish out of water, squished between vendors and pickpockets. But there was my soon-to-be husband, ready to shoot daggers at anyone who dared glance my way.

At the hotel, surrounded by bowls of fried masala peanuts and soft drinks, we dived into the real issues of inter-state marriage. There were no mountains too high for us to climb together. His culinary skills were top-notch—he could whip up a feast while I was still trying to master the art of boiling water. That pretty much settled my worries about cooking. And I was more than willing to learn from him. Dining out would always be an option, we agreed.

Then came the big reveal—he confessed that he had written the response to my matrimonial ad, signing it as his father, just as I had done. We burst into laughter, two partners in crime bonded by our shared audacity. It felt good to know we both had a mischievous streak!

After quite a bit of family drama, we tied the knot on December 6, 1975. With guest control orders in place, I didn't invite any colleagues, nor did he invite his, except for a handful of close friends—after all, this wasn't exactly a lavish Bollywood wedding. The spread was strictly vegetarian to honour the groom's family preferences and habits. Starkly different to what is served at Bengali weddings, so, I guess, no one missed not being invited. I touched my parents' feet, tears in my eyes when leaving home, and saw a glimmer of emotion in Baba's eyes—something I had never witnessed at my siblings' weddings.

As I slid into the flower-adorned car, a wave of sadness swept over me—a gentle reminder of the life I was leaving behind. It felt as though I was stepping away from my family to embrace a new one. For a moment, a question flickered in my mind: "Am I abandoning my parents?"

But I paused and let my heart speak. This wasn't abandonment—it was the beginning of a new chapter. Isn't it natural for women to carve out their own paths, to embrace the joys of marriage and motherhood and to weave their unique essence into the fabric of life? I reminded myself that my parents had raised me to be strong and independent and to seek love, happiness and fulfilment in my journey ahead.

With each mile the car travelled, I could feel the warmth of my family's love surrounding me, cheering me on from behind. This was not just my story; it was an evolution of all our stories, a new chapter filled with hope and promise. I was not leaving them behind; I was carrying their love with me, ready to weave it into the fabric of my new life. And in that realization, my heart swelled with excitement for the adventures that lay ahead.

The ride from my parental home to my husband's was a memorable adventure, one that would certainly earn its place in the annals of our marriage. Squeezed between my new husband and his younger brother in the back seat of a friend's Fiat and just when we thought we were in the clear, fate decided to play a little trick on us— the car broke down near Park Circus. Cue the panic! How on earth were we going to make it home in time for the 'mahurat,' the auspicious moment set for our grand welcome? It felt like the universe was testing us. Can you imagine- a bride, all decked out in her finery, standing on the sidewalk, hair perfectly coiffed and makeup flawless, waiting for a taxi that seemed to be on a permanent coffee break?

After several failed attempts at flagging down a cab—some drivers pretending not to see us, others speeding past with barely a glance— an elderly *Sardarji*(a term of address/reference for a Sikh) pulled over. The moment he spotted us, his face lit up with a mix of amusement and concern. It was as if he had stumbled upon a scene from a comedy show: a newly married couple stranded on the roadside, looking like we'd just stepped out of a Bollywood film. As we piled into his cab, I couldn't help but chuckle at the absurdity of it all. Here we were, fresh from the altar, and already facing the kind of mishap that would make for great stories in the years to come. As the *Sardarji* navigated the traffic, he shot us a warm smile and said, "Don't worry, *beta* (an endearing term for children), we'll make it in time." And just like that, what could have been a disaster turned into one of the most humorous and endearing moments of our journey together.

Arriving home, we were met with concerned looks from my in-laws, a contrast to the whirlwind of excitement we had just escaped. Then came the shocker the following day with my husband announcing we would be going on a honeymoon in two days. In 1975, this was practically revolutionary! Newlyweds were usually expected to stay home and get acquainted with family members.

"We're going, tickets are booked!" he announced, boldly defying tradition. After a bit of grumbling, they gave in. With our packed suitcases and a wave of goodbye to the in-laws—who were hugely disappointed by our blatant disregard for convention—we set off on our first adventure, fully prepared for whatever chaos the universe had in store for us.

Our honeymoon was a delightful mix of sweet and salty—miscalculating the budget, running out of cash, and encountering a distant relative who came to our rescue, handing us a bundle of notes as if we were on a reality show. And there we were, surrounded by beautiful scenery, standing by the still waters of the *Mirik Lake* (Lake in Darjeeling), shivering in the cold, without adequate woollens, staring at the snow-capped Kanchenjunga Mountain range. Forty-nine years later, leafing through the wedding albums brings on a rush of memories, sweet, quirky, and hilarious.

Coming first to the hilarious part. It all began the night we spent in *Kalimpong*, in a colonial bungalow that we thought was haunted—or so we believed at the time. The atmosphere was straight out of a gothic novel: creaking floorboards, flickering candlelight, and a cold draft that made the hairs on the back of our necks stand up. After a long day of exploring the hill station, we retired for the night, only to be jolted awake by strange noises echoing through the halls.

“What on earth is that?” I whispered, clutching my husband’s arm as the sounds grew more distinct. A mix of eerie whispers, soft thuds, and the unmistakable creak of old wood—this was way out of a typical hotel stay. We exchanged anxious glances, half convinced we’d been checked into a haunted house.

“Maybe it’s just the wind,” he said, trying to ease my growing unease. But as the night wore on, the noises became even more pronounced. A shadow flitted past the window, and I shot up in bed. “Did you see that?” I exclaimed. “We need to check this out! What if it’s a ghost?!”

Fuelled by a blend of curiosity and adrenaline, we decided to investigate. Armed only with flashlights, we crept down the hallway. The old portraits lining the walls seemed to watch us as we passed, their eyes frozen in time as if they knew something we didn’t.

When we turned a corner, a loud crash from the kitchen startled us both. We froze, exchanging terrified glances. “Should we go in?” I asked, my heart pounding.

“Only if you want to be the first couple haunted on your honeymoon!” he joked, trying to lighten the mood.

Finally, we pushed open the kitchen door and to our surprise, the culprit wasn’t a ghost at all. An owl, having squeezed in through an open window, was knocking over pots and pans in search of snacks. "It’s a mountain scops owl!" I laughed, both relieved and amused.

Just then, the caretaker appeared, chuckling at our antics. “Ah, the nocturnal birds of *Kalimpong*,” he teased. “You’re not the first to be spooked by the local wildlife.”

As we calmed down, he shared some of the bungalow's history. "Many guests have claimed to hear strange noises," he explained. "But it's mostly the wind playing tricks. This place has its stories—of old lovers, grand feasts, and yes, a particularly mischievous mountain owl."

Feeling a mix of embarrassment and intrigue, we returned to our room. The rest of the night passed without incident, except for the occasional hoot of the unwelcome nocturnal visitor.

The next morning, as we checked out, the caretaker offered one final titbit. "But we do have a ghost tour in town if you're interested!" he said with a wink.

"Next time!", we laughed, relieved that our romantic getaway hadn't turned into a horror story. As we drove away, we realized the real twist was yet to come. In our excitement, we had left our camera on the mantlepiece. When we turned back to retrieve it, we caught a glimpse of the owl peering out from its perch on the old Oak tree, almost as if saying "Good riddance to bad rubbish!" Those saucer-like eyes seemed to have caught a whiff of something suspicious. The beak? A tiny, pointy smirk, as though trying to suppress a chuckle at our expense. Add to that, those stiff, "I-mean-business" eyebrows: a perfect combination of wisdom and sass wrapped in feathers.

Nearly five decades later, we still chuckle when we meet honeymooners, eager to hear their stories. Often, they'll remark, "You two are such an inspiration!" as they watch us enthusiastically dive into activities typically reserved for younger couples. Their faces light up with admiration, and we graciously accept the compliment.

Inside, I smile to myself, reflecting on how that leap into marriage—sometimes taken with a blind curve—has led us to such an extraordinary adventure. Life has a funny way of surprising us, and I wouldn't change a thing about our journey together. Every twist, every turn, has added richness to our story, and sharing that story with others is a joy in itself.

Awkward moments

My first visit to my *sasural*, my husband's family home, is filled with memories sweet, sour and incredibly funny. The purpose was to meet relatives who hadn't attended our wedding and to be introduced to the extended family. While the occasion was meant to be celebratory, I sensed a subtle undercurrent of disappointment about our inter-state marriage. Only a handful of relatives came to greet the new bride, while others visited out of curiosity, eager to see what a working woman looked like. Some left with sceptical expressions, perhaps wondering how I would fit into their traditional family.

One comment that stayed with me came from my husband's teacher; a man firmly rooted in old-world values. With genuine curiosity, he asked, "*What made you marry a girl from another community?*" This question echoed a sentiment shared by many in the family and among colleagues. Having grown up in a diverse environment, I had assumed—rather naively—that my transition into this new life would be effortless. But reality proved otherwise.

There were customs to observe and adjustments to make. Initially, these unfamiliar traditions felt overwhelming, and I worried about unintentionally offending anyone. Yet, as I navigated this new cultural landscape, I began to understand the deep significance behind these practices. Embracing them, even during our infrequent visits, allowed me to appreciate the richness of their values while introducing my perspectives in a gentle, gradual way.

This process transformed my relationship with my in-laws. What once felt daunting evolved into a journey of mutual understanding and respect. Immersing myself in their traditions opened my mind and heart in ways I hadn't anticipated. I learned that customs, while deeply rooted, aren't rigid; they can adapt and coexist. Over time, I stopped seeing our differences as obstacles and instead embraced them as opportunities to learn and grow. This shift strengthened our bond and created a more harmonious atmosphere. We celebrated not only our heritages but also the unique blend that emerged from them.

In time, I felt surrounded by genuine warmth and protection from my new family. This meant everything to me. The initial barriers that had existed before our marriage, broke down following long discussions on our differences, deepening our understanding of one another. I particularly cherished the summer nights on the terrace, sitting on *charpais*—woven beds—listening to the lively chatter and playful banter among siblings. Those moments of shared laughter and camaraderie were priceless, teaching me that blending traditions and forging new relationships can create something truly beautiful.

It reminds me that love and respect can transcend cultural boundaries, fostering deeper connections that are rooted in understanding and appreciation.

One evening, when a sudden craving for sweet *lassi* (yoghurt drink) struck, one of the siblings dashed off to the local '*Halwai*' (sweet shop) and returned with a big tumbler of the drink with chunks of ice, served chilled in mud cups that carried the delightful scent of petrichor. As we sipped from our cups, I felt at ease. Integrating with my new family felt easier. Seeing us off at the railway station with teary eyes, at the end of each visit, felt like being wrapped in their love and affection.

It wasn't exactly a well-kept secret that I had never set foot in the kitchen. I definitely didn't fit the "*Bhabi*" (sister-in-law) mould from those dramatic Hindi TV soap operas, depicted as homely-comely women, cooking and serving meals, and then magically cleaning up without breaking a sweat. Neither was I the 'sit-in-the-courtyard-and-knit' type—knitting, sewing, or embroidering. I couldn't do any to save my life. Let's just say my crafting skills were somewhere between 'non-existent' and 'hazardous.'

Therefore, initially, I felt a little out of place—and maybe a smidge embarrassed. So, I did what any self-respecting non-cook would do: volunteered to wash dishes and chop vegetables. And lo and behold, over the years, I earned the affectionate title of the family '*Bai*' (dishwasher)! But occasionally I surprised them with a dish or two, slowly but surely proving that I could at least not burn down the kitchen. It took some time, but eventually, they began to accept me as I was, minus the skills of a typical housewife.

After marriage, both of us faced our own set of challenges at work. Some of my colleagues, particularly from the Bengali community, were quick to label me a non-conformist. I vividly remember overhearing a conversation among senior colleagues about my marriage: "Were there no good Bengali boys that she had to marry outside her community?" Such comments revealed a narrow-mindedness that failed to appreciate the diversity of cultures that make up our society. At my husband's workplace, colleagues also commented, "So, you married a Bengali girl?" Quick-witted as ever, he shut them down with a simple, confident reply: "I married a girl. Period."

Amidst navigating cultural perceptions, we were also grappling with a significant life decision: whether to remain in India or consider immigrating to Canada. My husband had received two PhD scholarship offers, one from the University of Waterloo and another from a professor relocating to Berkeley, both promising exciting opportunities. However, after much deliberation, he chose to turn them down. Our commitment to our ageing parents was paramount; we felt it was important to be present for them during their sunset years.

I often wonder how our lives might have unfolded differently if we had moved to the West in 1977. Job opportunities would likely have been abundant, but I would have missed out on so much—especially the close bond I shared with Baba and Ma. They depended on me emotionally, just as I relied on them for their advice and guidance. Being married did not end this mutual reliance; instead, it deepened my sense of responsibility towards them.

One of my greatest joys was sending a small monthly allowance to my parents. It was my way of expressing gratitude for the sacrifices they made to provide me with the best upbringing and education they could afford. Choosing to stay back and care for my parents was one of the most fulfilling decisions we made as a couple. It wasn't an easy choice, but knowing I could offer them the support and comfort they deserved brought me an enduring sense of well-being and purpose.

As I reflect on how far we've come, I am overcome with nostalgia for those who laid the foundation for our brighter future. It's deeply ironic—despite all we've achieved, there's an undeniable sense of inadequacy, knowing they're no longer here to share these moments. The joy of success is often tempered by a lingering ache for the stories and laughter that could have filled our homes if they had been part of this journey.

This truth brings both gratitude and sadness. The comforts and opportunities I enjoy today are poignant reminders of their absence, yet their sacrifices inspire me to live by the values they instilled—resilience, gratitude, and the importance of family. Though they aren't here to witness this chapter, I feel their presence guiding me.

Honouring their legacy means cherishing what they gave us, embracing the life we've built, and making the most of every moment with those we love. Their dreams and spirit continue to fuel my motivation, reminding me that the best way to pay tribute to them is to carry their values forward.

Like many marriages, ours has faced its share of challenges—ranging from heated arguments to silent standoffs. Back then, marriage was seen as a lifelong commitment—a partnership meant to endure both joy and adversity. I still recall those playful banter that sometimes escalated into verbal duels, leaving me stubbornly retreating to bed on an empty stomach. My husband, on the other hand, had a different approach. "*You do what you wish. I'm not skipping dinner over a silly argument,*" ... his mantra.

I'll never forget one particular evening after a quarrel when I found a packet of biscuits by my bedside—his way of extending an unspoken truce. Initially, I resisted, pride warring with hunger, but eventually, hunger won. That small gesture, humorous in hindsight, taught me some valuable lessons: never go to bed hungry (acid reflux is a cruel teacher), always strive to reconcile before sleep and prioritize open communication to resolve conflicts effectively.

While I'm no marriage counsellor, I'd like to share a few insights that have helped us weather turbulent times. One of the most crucial early decisions we made was to avoid revisiting the past. When we first got to know each other, we agreed to focus on the present and build a future together, leaving behind the baggage of previous experiences. This approach may not work for everyone, but for us, it kept unnecessary resentments at bay. Honesty became the foundation of our relationship. Even amidst serious arguments, we never lost our sense of humour.

Today, the landscape of marriage looks very different. The notion of permanence in relationships has evolved significantly, with societal attitudes shifting to accept divorce as a valid choice rather than a failure. Economic independence has empowered modern women to prioritize their happiness and walk away from unhealthy relationships, unshackled by the stigma of being "divorced." A big departure from our days. What's more, it's heartening to see parents today actively supporting their daughters in leaving abusive relationships, often welcoming them back into the family fold with the same warmth and enthusiasm as when they first left home. This cultural shift is a testament to the growing emphasis on individual happiness and well-being over rigid societal expectations.

In this evolving narrative, the definition of commitment is being reimagined. While every relationship will inevitably face its share of storms, the ultimate goal should always be mutual respect, emotional fulfilment, and the freedom to make choices that align with one's authentic self. Whether someone chooses to stay or leave, the focus must remain on fostering a life of dignity, happiness, and personal growth—free from the shadow of fear or judgment.

Births

1979 was a year of profound significance with the arrival of our firstborn. The first granddaughter of both sides of the family. But the journey to motherhood, was a mix of exhilaration and nerves, like riding a rollercoaster down a blind curve. During those nine months, my colleagues, many of whom were already mothers, became my biggest cheerleaders. They indulged my cravings for Pork Sorpotel, spicy crab curry, and various Goan dishes I loved but never learned to cook. Concomitant to the work ethics, pregnant employees received special treatment. Footrests magically appeared under desks, workloads were adjusted, and the pantry boy became my best friend, frequently serving tall glasses of sweet, icy-cold coffee. Those little luxuries still make me smile, a testament to the caring organizational culture I was lucky to experience.

When my maternity leave began, I carried their good wishes like a talisman. Admittedly, I was bracing for the worst after hearing enough horror stories about labour to fuel a lifetime of nightmares. But the reality turned out quite differently. Four days before my due date, I was admitted to Woodlands Nursing Home at 7 p.m. As I was wheeled into the labour room, the nurses told my husband that it would be a long night before the baby would make an appearance, advising him to go home and rest. Reluctantly, he left.

Contrary to their predictions, four hours later—just two minutes before midnight—our daughter made her grand entrance. My banshee-like screams, loud enough to threaten the hospital's glass windows, were instantly replaced by awe and joy when I first saw her. There she was, my six-pound, six-ounce carbon copy of her father, lying in a kidney-shaped tray as if saying, *"Hello, so you're my mom. Let's see what you've got!"* My tears flowed freely, a mix of relief, joy, and gratitude.

Postpartum blues? Not a chance. I was too busy imagining her future to dwell on anything else. When she was placed in my arms for the first time, an overwhelming wave of emotions hit me like a tsunami. My tears dripped onto her tiny face, and just then, my husband walked in, grinning like a Cheshire Cat, looking two inches taller with pride. *"Look at her! A chip off the old block!"* he exclaimed. My parents echoed the sentiment: *"Oh my, she's a mini version of him!"*

Five days later, we brought our bundle of joy home, where the real adventure awaited. At the door stood Ma, beaming with pride and ready to welcome her first granddaughter. *"You need to rest and recover,"* she said, gently taking the pink bundle from my arms. I couldn't help but chuckle. After days in the nursing home filled with nourishing meals, ample sleep, and only a few interruptions for feeding, I felt more rested than I had in months. Still, seeing her confidence and love was a relief. Her decision to take over was a lifeline. Her presence was a calming force as I stumbled into the uncertain role of a new mother.

This was her first grandparenting experience and she embraced it with enthusiasm, having missed the chance with her two grandsons from my older sisters. I was in for a well-orchestrated stage play, on the sixth day when she prepared for my daughter's first bath like a pro. Everything was laid out perfectly: towels, Johnson's Baby products, olive oil, a tiny outfit, and a neatly folded triangular nappy. Sitting on the floor with her saree hitched up to her knees, she positioned my daughter securely between her legs and when I saw the half-dried umbilical cord dangling from my daughter's navel, I panicked. *"Don't worry,"* Ma said with a reassuring smile. *"It'll fall off in a few days."* Phew! Why hadn't anyone at the nursing home warned me about this?

Act I, Scene 1... first came the oil massage: crossing, twisting, bending, flexing—my heart raced with every manoeuvre. What if something fell apart? Then, flipping her like an omelette for the back rub! I was completely awed by Ma's dexterity; I knew I would have dropped my slippery eel of a baby in a heartbeat.

Act I, Scene 2...the sponge bath and head wash making my head spin. Cupping my daughter's tiny head, Ma carefully poured water, expertly avoiding her eyes, ears, and nostrils. After drying, talcuming, and applying homemade kajal—a perfect black dot on the cheek—my beautifully packaged doll was handed back to me for feeding.

Watching Ma take charge with such ease was humbling and heartwarming. Her wisdom, patience, and unwavering support made all the difference, transforming a daunting phase of life into a cherished memory filled with laughter, love, and growth.

When I returned to work after three months of maternity leave, I felt at ease knowing my daughter was in the best hands—my mother's.

February **1983**, and I was preparing for round two. The drama resumed with me driving through deserted Calcutta streets in a friend's broken-down jalopy at 2 a.m. This time, I felt more at ease. When I was wheeled into the labour room, I saw my gynaecologist's reassuring smile and thought, "Here we go again! Another round of shrieking contest?".

At 7:05 a.m., my second daughter popped out without much fuss, just a feeble cry after a few gentle pats. The nurse handed her to me, bottoms up, looking like a skinned chicken, and proclaimed, "Look, you have another beautiful daughter!" I was too overwhelmed by her magic to comprehend the nurse's odd presentation at the time.

Later, my husband shared his side of the story, recounting the panic he felt when the doctor and his assistant rushed out of the theatre, avoiding him completely. Alarm bells went off in his head: Had something gone wrong? Then, a matron in a spotless white uniform approached him and asked him to follow her. "Can you come with me, Sir?" she said, leading him to her office. He sat down, all confused. "Your firstborn is a girl?" she began. "Yes," he replied. "I'm sorry to say, your second child is also a girl?" the matron announced, barely a whisper.

His mind raced as he tried to process the situation. "What's going on?". Why is she sorry?", he thought, stifling laughter while reassuring her that he was perfectly fine with having another daughter, not in the know-how, the hospital staff had become overly cautious after encountering parents who outright refused to accept female children. Apparently, they had faced their fair share of melodramatic reactions—parents bursting into tears as if the doctor had personally decided to deliver a girl!

Later, during our post-delivery visits, we couldn't help but confront the doctor about his hasty exit from the operating room. He sheepishly admitted that he had been cornered by some very disappointed parents as if, he somehow controlled the gender of the babies he delivered. "Look, I just handle the delivery!" he chuckled, throwing his hands up in mock surrender. We erupted into laughter at the absurdity of it all.

It was a light-hearted reminder of the biases that still lingered, but we also took the opportunity to celebrate the joy of our daughters—who, let's be honest, were always destined to rule the household! Today, we stand proud, delighted by their achievements and honoured to see them both thrive as incredibly successful women in their respective fields.

As a second-time mother, I thought I'd finally earn the right to bathe my infant. No way. Ma took it upon herself to do this activity. So be it! During my three months of maternity leave, I remained an audience member, witnessing the same hour-long bathing ritual that sometimes stretched on in the winter sunshine for that all-important dose of Vitamin D. It wasn't until my daughters were over two that I was trusted with bucket baths, and even then, only under her watchful eye.

When my grandchildren arrived, I was relieved to be spared from the bathing duties. What did I know? I only had Ma's traditional methods to draw from, which would have certainly been deemed outmoded in today's world of modern baby bathing gadgets.

I often pull out those fond memories of Ma's knee baths, a cherished part of my archives. I wish she were here to see and hold her great-grandchildren. I know she would have adored that role as much as she loved being '*Didima*' (maternal grandmother) to her granddaughters. Through all the chaos and uncertainty of motherhood, I am forever grateful to Ma for guiding me with her wisdom, humour, and unyielding love.

Parenting (hair-raising moments)

Though I had read Dr Spock's book on raising newborns, nothing could prepare me for the crises that would inevitably arise. My mother, however, handled these situations with an effortless grace that left us all in awe. I vividly recall the day when my little one, a curious toddler, had taken a fistful of puffed rice and suddenly began choking, her face turning a terrifying shade of blue. Panic gripped us as we wrung our hands in despair. But then Ma swooped in, her instincts kicking in like a well-rehearsed dance. She picked the child up, turned her upside down, and with a firm smack on her back, out came the soggy rice ball. Relief washed over me as I cried out, overwhelmed by gratitude. At that moment, Ma showed me the strength of a mother's love, while I felt utterly lost, paralysed by fear.

We still chuckle about the nightly dramas with the older one. Hubby had to serenade her before bed with her all-time favourite song... "*Sohag chand bodoni dhoni...Nacho to dekhi...bala nacho to dekhi.*" (Bengali song translated to read as "O' moon bodied well-endowed beauty, dance for me to see. O' lady, dance for me to see. O' lady, dance for me to see...source internet). Picture this: a tiny goddess dancing on her bed like a whirling dervish, spinning in circles until we thought we'd need a GPS to find her. Some nights, it felt like we were trapped in an endless encore, with her demanding more songs. Late-night snacks? Ha! Those were mere distractions, like trying to lure a cat away from a laser pointer. Bread butter jam would be served, cut in manageable portions to bite on, while the musical soiree continued. Next day at work? Let's say our exhausted faces invited more comments than a viral meme and I wanted to shout out... "Gosh, if only you experienced what we did last night, you'd be napping in your chair, drooling like a toddler!"

As the years passed, a new challenge came: the dreaded binky. My little one had grown so attached to her pacifier that it seemed to be an extension of her body. It was her constant companion while sleeping, tucked snugly in her mouth like a beloved friend. But the time had come to bid farewell to the binky, and I knew it was not going to be easy.

Hubby and I strategized, drawing on every trick in the parenting book. We tried the typical approach: "Big girls don't need binkies!" But my toddler's eyes, filled with unwavering loyalty to her pacifier, told me she wasn't buying it. It became clear that we'd need a more creative solution.

That's when Ma stepped in again, her maternal wisdom never failing to impress. "Why don't we tell her a little story?" she suggested with a twinkle in her eye. And so began the tale of the "Binky Bandit"—an imaginary bogeyman who roamed the night, snatching away binkies from kids who didn't give them up. We painted a vivid picture of this mysterious figure, a shadowy, mischievous creature who would appear out of nowhere to whisk away pacifiers forever, making it a "no-return" policy.

One evening, after a particularly dramatic rendition of the story, we told our daughter that the Binky Bandit would come for her beloved pacifier if she didn't leave it on the window sill before bed. We emphasized the "no-take-backs" rule, that the bandit would not return what he took. She seemed to take it seriously, but there was a catch: she wasn't about to let go without a fight. Still, there was a spark of curiosity in her eyes—like she was testing us.

The first night, we placed the binky on the sill together, nervously awaiting what might unfold. She struggled to fall asleep without it. To our astonishment, she woke up in the middle of the night, went to the window, and stood there, peering into the dark as if expecting to see the Binky Bandit himself. After a long pause, she slowly turned and came back to bed, eyes wide but without her pacifier. She had missed noticing it on the window sill. "I think the bandit took it," she whispered a little thrill in her voice.

The second night, she didn't ask for the binky, though we had a 'standby' in case of a full-blown meltdown. But she surprised us. There was no protest, no tantrum. Instead, she looked at us, grinning like she'd just outwitted the greatest villain. "I'm a big girl now!" she declared proudly, drifting off to sleep to the singing of lullabies. From that moment on, the pacifier was nothing more than a distant memory.

As for us, we revelled in the peace of no more late-night binky hunts. The binky saga became a fond family tale, told with laughter during dinner, reminding us of how, sometimes, the most creative strategies—like a mythical bogeyman—can work wonders in the most unexpected ways. Looking back, I think the real bandit in this story was the binky itself, slowly but surely stealing our sleep—and our sanity—until it finally vanished.

We were not spared of the younger one's stage plays, which had the whole household spinning like we were in a circus. One evening, Ma heroically stopped her from dashing out the door to greet her dad, his briefcase precariously swinging in one hand while he juggled a grocery bag in the other. It was like a scene from a comedy sketch. Cue the pandemonium! In protest, or pain, whatever...she let out a wail that could probably be heard from space. “Did I dislocate her arm?” Ma kept asking, panic-stricken. It was like a scene from a sitcom, with her crying like a needle stuck in a gramophone record, while we scrambled to find a paediatric clinic.

The waiting rooms were packed, each child more boisterous than the last, while we endured the melodrama of our own little star. Visits to three clinics yielded nothing, after checking out her arm, shoulder, and elbow. Finally, at the last clinic of the night, which was about to close, we managed to persuade the receptionist to squeeze us in— "Our child is in acute pain," we said, barely concealing our desperation. The doctor took a quick look at her arm and sent us on our way with a clean bill of health, declaring nothing was wrong. It was as if she knew the magic words because she stopped crying the instant we walked out. But who knows? The problem may have been resolved with the bending and flexing of the arm at the clinics, as we think back to that nightmarish incident.

Ah, the summer of 1985—what a scorcher! One of those blistering Sundays when the fan was working overtime, valiantly attempting to blow away the oppressive heat. The whole family had gathered around the dining table, seeking solace in frosty drinks. The girls were happily indulging in their newfound love, Nestlé's market-testing freebie: iced tea "Paloma." Meanwhile, hubby and I were savouring our grown-up summer cooler—refreshing gin with lime cordial served in frost-coated glasses, so picture-perfect, they could have graced the pages of a cocktail magazine.

Then, the day took an unexpectedly hilarious twist. Somehow, our two-year-old daughter—armed with the stealth of a seasoned spy—managed to sneak a few sips from one of our gin glasses. How she pulled it off remains a mystery, but toddlers have their ways.

As we polished off our drinks and reached for a refill, we glanced out at the balcony and saw her. There she was, our pint-sized party crasher, swaggering like a miniature diva, humming a merry tune. The unmistakable look of mischief danced across her face, and it didn't take a detective to figure out something was up.

"Did you drink from our glasses?" we asked, trying to stifle our laughter. With a goofy grin that could melt hearts, she proudly confessed, *"It was different... lemony!"* The innocent allure of that translucent potion had introduced her to the finer things in life.

Watching her prance around like a happy little gin connoisseur, we couldn't decide whether to laugh or panic. "*Well,*" my husband muttered, "*at least she has good taste.*" Summer had suddenly become a whole lot more entertaining—and a lesson learned: always keep the cocktails out of reach of curious tiny hands!

In hindsight, those hair-raising moments in parenting are what keep us laughing—because let's face it, if we didn't find humour in the chaos, we'd be in serious trouble! Parenting is the only job where your daily performance review is based on how well you handle impromptu concerts and stage meltdowns, all while desperately trying to stay awake.

Having two meant a load of weight in ensuring there was no sibling rivalry. A common challenge many families face. I was fortunate that my daughters navigated this phase with remarkable harmony. Reflecting on their relationship, I've learned that a parent's neutral stance is crucial in fostering a sense of fairness and equality. Children are incredibly perceptive; they can pick up on even the slightest cues that might suggest favouritism, which can lead to feelings of inferiority. We consciously tried to cultivate an environment where both children felt equally loved and valued.

This experience left me puzzled when I heard stories from other parents who had to be overly cautious, constantly managing jealousy and disputes among their children. I couldn't relate to their struggles, and it prompted me to reflect on the unique relationship my daughters had forged.

Communication has been the secret sauce in our family recipe! We kept the lines open, encouraging our daughters to share their feelings so they always felt heard and valued. When conflicts bubbled up—because let's be honest, sibling rivalry is practically a rite of passage—we stepped back, letting them tackle their disputes like mini mediators. It was all about empowering them to sort things out and reinforcing their sisterly bond.

But when tensions escalated and it felt like World War III was about to break out, hubby was appointed as the mediator... "Now, you be the judge!" This became our family punchline, often resurfacing in conversations about their childhood squabbles. Who knew that settling disputes could come with such a side serving of humour?

This crucial journey taught us that sibling rivalry isn't a given. With intentional parenting that emphasizes love, respect, and collaboration, it's possible to cultivate a lasting friendship between siblings that can withstand the test of time. By nurturing their bond, we've not only avoided many of the common pitfalls but also created a relationship built on trust and companionship—an invaluable gift that we hope will endure throughout their lives.

CHAPTER SIX

Echoes of Absence

In the quiet corners of my heart
Your laughter lingers, a bittersweet art
Whispers of moments never to be reclaimed
Each memory a flicker, each shadow a name

Walking through the hallways where memories bloom
Shadows of grief weave a tapestry of gloom
Photos on walls, frozen in time
Reminders of love that once felt sublime

Losses

Thakurma (grandmother)— In October of 1979, the family's grand matriarch, gracefully left the stage of life. Her passing struck with an incomprehensible force, shattering the dam of memories. She had been an integral part of my childhood, her presence shaping so many of my formative years. Every summer, she would arrive, bringing with her the essence of the season. Among her treasures was a *tokri* (cane basket) brimming with '*Langra*' mangoes, a variety first cultivated in Varanasi. Neatly arranged in layers and resting on beds of mango leaves, these sweet-and-tart delights became our all-time favourite. Alongside them, she would bring boxes of special '*Chom-Chom*' sweets—Indian desserts so uniquely delicious that no other *halwai* (confectioner) could ever match their taste or texture. These were carefully packed in boxes, double-wrapped in muslin, knotted at the top, and accompanied by her few personal belongings. And, of course, she never forgot the boxes of colourful glass bangles, adorned with twisted golden threads, which she picked up from the *Mughalsarai* station. These, and many other thoughtful gifts, were her way of showing love to her grandchildren.

The sound of the cycle bell ringing from the rickshaw announced her arrival from a distance. We would lean over the veranda railing, eagerly waiting to catch a glimpse of her white hair, white saree, and the white cotton shawl she always wrapped around her chest and head when she was outdoors. A fiercely independent woman, *Thakurma* firmly refused to let Baba pick her up from the railway station, responding with a resolute "NO!" Having travelled solo and with her children across the length and breadth of India, she was a seasoned traveller. Her stubborn streak only grew stronger as she moved from her fifties into her seventies and beyond.

Baba would wait by the gate, ready to greet her, helping unload the many-sized cloth bags and her battered tin trunk. It was clear from the state of her belongings that she had travelled far. The anti-theft pocket stitched into the waist of her petticoat, where she kept the cash, coins, and her cherished "*japer mala*" (prayer beads), was a testament to her caution and experience. After paying the rickshaw driver, she would enter the house, slightly dishevelled but full of life, her frail white arms opening wide for the big bear hugs we all eagerly awaited. Every summer, her presence made our home feel whole again.

Once the hugs and kisses were exchanged, Baba and Ma would touch her feet in respect. After a few hours of rest, fuelled by cups of milky, sugary tea, she would spring to action, rallying us four girls for a whirlwind of activities.

"*Khukhu*, I hope you've collected all the silver foils from your father's cigarette packets! This time, I'm going to create the Tree of Life!" she'd exclaim, turning to the eldest, who was responsible for gathering the foils and carefully pressing them between the pages of her heavy "*Gitanjali*" (the English translation of Tagore's poetry). The final creation, as always, was amazing. With her magical hands, she would roll, twist, and shape the foils, glueing them onto matchsticks to achieve the desired effect.

In compliance with her standing instructions, the older two siblings had spent the year collecting, washing and storing discarded clothes, sarees and kitchen mops in preparation for the next summer's craft project. After testing the fabric and designs, *Thakurma* would transform them into rag dolls and colourful *Kanthas* (hand-stitched throw rugs adorned with sequins), much to the envy of anyone who visited. From what seemed like scraps, she would create treasures—an ethnic-looking rag doll with beady eyes and long braids, which remained my constant companion until my teenage years. None of us ever inherited her incredible creativity, but we cherished every moment spent in her enchanting presence.

We never tired of listening to stories from her childhood—her marriage at the age of twelve, playing hopscotch with her stepdaughter, who was just two years younger than her, and then becoming a mother by the time she turned thirteen. These stories, so foreign to our ears, often left us in awe. Despite being widowed in her thirties and left to raise six sons on her widow's pension, she showed no sign of regret. Fortunately, her stepdaughters and biological daughter had been married off before tragedy struck. Her sons-in-law, both of whom were well-placed in the legal profession, helped whenever she needed assistance with property matters.

Thakurma's true experience of 'living' began only after her sons were married and she had the joy of welcoming grandchildren. It was then that she expressed a desire to settle in Kashi (Varanasi), her second home. Although her family resisted, she had her way. In Kashi, the "little lady" spread her wings and grew stronger. She travelled to Kailash, Uttarkashi, Amarnath, and Rameshwaram in her pursuit of spirituality, sometimes alone and sometimes accompanied by my '*Mejo Pishi*' (father's elder middle sister). When the summer temperatures in Varanasi soared, she would grace us with her presence, filling our home with her warmth and energy.

During one of our conversations, which happened mostly at bedtime, I asked... '*Thamma, how come you can read, write, and know the Ramayan and Mahabharata end to end and also deliver babies, without any formal education?*' Her response still rings in my ears. *"There is nothing one cannot achieve if the mind, body, and soul speak the same language".*

"*And what is that language?*" curiosity made me ask. "*Determination to overcome all the odds*", is what she replied. She had mastered that 'oneness' and achieved what many in her generation would not have dared to even contemplate doing.

Her journey towards self-growth didn't have any end. Self-taught, she was a prolific reader and writer, possessed with unparalleled humaneness, which extended to the animal world as well. The latter made real by recounting her experience with delivering a calf.

As the story goes, there was a pregnant cow in the neighbour's cowshed mooing in pain. *Thamma aka Thakurma*, was called in for help fearing the cow and calf would not survive. Unnerved, she went to the cowshed late at night and calmed '*Moni*', the Moo, with her soothing touches, while inserting her right hand into her uterus only to discover that the calf was in breach position. Again, it was her magic hands that gently manoeuvred the calf's head into position, thereby easing the delivery. Both cow and calf became her lifelong friends, sidling up to her whenever she came to visit them. It was her confidence that made her explore the unknown and in turn, gain the confidence of others.

Her indomitable spirit, her courage, her in-depth knowledge, and her social skills, are all testimony of her greatness. A fiercely independent lady, even in death she had her way. "I will die in my husband's '*bheeta*' (home) where I came as a bride. The family's ancestral home for three generations, was her last resting place, refusing to be hospitalized and refusing to stay with any of her sons. The matriarch died a peaceful death in her sleep in 1979 on the auspicious day of Durga Puja, at the age somewhere around 85/ 86, is my best guess. Most people are inspired by famous leaders, authors, poets, and freedom fighters. *Thamma* remains my inspiration, my muse. There is a separate file full of her memories, which I dip into, from time to time.

To say she was beautiful would be an understatement. She was regal, as befitting her regal ancestry. We only got to know of this much later by happenstance, reading without permission, Baba's responses to matrimonial ads, with an entire paragraph explaining the ancestry of the family and of the matriarch being a descendent of the famous Indian novelist and poet of Bengal of the 18th century. There were no records to validate her claim, except from facts gathered during her growing up years, filtered down the generations.

Another 'who's who' of her rich ancestry emerged quite by accident. As was customary, on the third day after our wedding, my in-laws proposed a visit to *Kalighat temple*—a renowned Hindu temple dedicated to Goddess Kali—to seek the Goddess's blessings for our new life. To ensure a smooth and swift *darshan* (viewing of the deity), *Thakurma* had penned a note with instructions to meet her maternal brother, who lived within the temple premises.

That note uncovered yet another branch of her lineage: the descendants of the Halder family, once the owners of the Kalighat temple. Following her directions, we located her maternal brother's home within the temple precincts. He turned out to be a tall, fair, strapping priest, his muscular frame and magnetic presence exuding a quiet authority.

Upon reading the note, he broke into a warm smile, instantly recognizing the connection. With an air of familial pride, he led us straight to the sanctum sanctorum, bypassing the usual queues. In an extraordinary gesture, he physically lifted my 42-kilogram frame to help me reach the feet of the Goddess—a privilege that only the head priest could bestow. That moment was magical: the flickering oil lamps cast a golden glow on the intricately adorned idol, the air heavy with the mingled fragrances of incense and flowers, and the rhythmic chants enveloping us in a divine embrace.

This exceptional favour, granted in deference to *Thakurma's* note, was never repeated. It marked a rare and unforgettable slice of her ancestry brought to life, etched forever in my memory.

With her passing, I lost the last of my grandparents—my beloved

Thakurma, who was more than family; she was my anchor and guide.

Didi (eldest sister)— On a frigid December day the same year, tragedy struck again, stealing away a cherished soul far too young. When the news of *Didi's* passing reached us, it felt as if the very ground beneath me had crumbled. My parents were shattered, their grief palpable, as the weight of loss enveloped our entire family. From four siblings, we were suddenly reduced to three—a cruel twist of fate that left an unshakeable ache in my gut.

Memories flooded my mind, overwhelming and relentless: *Didi,* radiant in her wedding saree, stepping into a new life with her husband; the pride in her eyes as she cradled her firstborn; laughter and love woven into the fabric of our shared moments. Then came the stark contrast—the haunting image of her lying motionless, mouth slightly ajar, eyes forever closed. The sight of her being carried away, borne on the shoulders of those who loved her, etched a profound emptiness in our hearts, leaving a chasm that would never be filled.

Her twelve-year-old son, once so vibrant and full of life, was suddenly left to grapple with the devastating loss of his mother. A heavy gloom settled over our family, casting a shadow that seemed impossible to lift. My brother-in-law, who had always been more like a brother to me and a son to my parents, retreated into himself, cutting off all connections and withdrawing completely from those around him.

This phase of our lives was marked by a heavy sadness that weighed down my parents, a burden they never truly recovered from. Their stoic expressions told the story—silent witnesses to their pain. They were hurting deeply after *Didi's* passing in December 1979. Each day felt like a reminder of the love that had been lost and the family ties that had frayed. The heartache lingers, echoing in the silence where laughter used to be, and I often find myself struggling with the ache of that absence, wishing we could have held on to what once was—not just her, but her family too.

When a loved one departs, the feelings that accompany their absence can be profound and multifaceted. Initially, there's often a sharp jolt of disbelief, a moment when the reality of their absence doesn't quite sink in. Then follows the waves of grief washing over, which feels both familiar and foreign. It's a visceral ache, a reminder of the bond you shared, now altered forever. As the days pass, a complex tapestry of emotions begins to unfold. Sadness takes centre stage, but it's often accompanied by feelings of anger, confusion, or even guilt and being confronted with questions that have no answers: Did I say everything I needed to say? Could I have done more? The "what ifs" linger like shadows, adding to the weight of loss.

1990 – Life Upended

1990 was a year that made our life turn turtle. My husband faced mounting pressure to relocate to another city to head the company's IT division. Caught in a whirlwind of uncertainty, he kept delaying the decision. As a stop-gap arrangement, he compromised to working five days a week at the new location, returning home for the weekends. A compromise we found was exhausting for him and us. And although tiring, it seemed the best solution. With our daughters thriving at Loreto House, one of Calcutta's premier schools, and my eighteen years of dedicated service at Nestlé, the thought of uprooting everything felt unbearable. What if the girls couldn't find a school of equal standing? What job prospects would await me in another city? The company's lack of a local office left me feeling adrift, my continuity of service hanging by a thread. Though I was assured a position if I returned, it felt like a meagre comfort. Transitioning from a two-income household to a single income was a bitter pill to swallow, despite the attractively packaged promotion.

Then, in June, another shock pierced through our fragile stability. My siblings and I were planning our parents' 50th wedding anniversary, set for July 15. We eagerly discussed the menu: Baba's favourite *kosha mangsho* (goat meat curry) and Ma's beloved *hasher deemer dalna* (duck egg curry) topped the list. We had planned for the exchange of rings and garlands, kept secret, to be unveiled closer to the date.

But life had other plans.

On Saturday, June 2, 1990, the shrill ring of the phone shattered the air, leaving me breathless as I rushed to answer. A voice heavy with grief delivered the devastating news: Baba, at seventy-six and seemingly healthy, had passed away in his sleep at his home away from the city. His friends, who had come to take him for their customary morning walk, found his door locked. Breaking in, they discovered he had journeyed to a new realm. The shock left me frozen, the enormity of the news crashing over me like a tidal wave.

Breaking the news to Ma was the hardest task I had ever faced. It felt surreal as we prepared to drive the 213 kilometres, our lunch plans from Saturday Club—a feast of fish kababs and chicken rolls—untouched. All our hopes for the anniversary celebration evaporated in an instant.

By the time we reached Baba's home, the cremation was over. My nephew had already performed the last rites in our absence, and we were left deprived of the final glance at Baba's body, unable to pay our last respects. It felt so much like him—to slip away without notice, leaving us grappling with the emptiness of his departure.

We returned to Calcutta with heavy hearts, carrying only a handful of mementoes: his well-worn sleeveless sweater, a Kashmiri shawl, and the soft brown linen chador he used to keep warm while sleeping. These stay with me along with his many antique fountain pens, engineering instruments and cameras, gifted to me during various phases of his life. This act of giving away his valuable possessions, spoke volumes of the life he chose, once his responsibilities were over—one of austerity and detachment. Material wealth meant little to him; years ago, he had renounced his rightful share of the ancestral home to support his younger brother, who had been stricken by polio. None of us contested his decision; his selflessness commanded our respect. "God will take care of him and his family," he often said, with a quiet conviction I could never fully embrace. Yet, I admired him deeply—for his unwavering faith, his wisdom, and the love he showered on us as a father, friend, teacher, and in my eyes, a living dictionary.

Even now, the mystery of his passing lingers in my mind, unanswerable and haunting. Did he sense the end approaching? Did he surrender to life's inevitability, believing karma had come full circle? A practitioner of Tantrism, he had spent his final years immersed in rituals and meditation, seeking liberation through knowledge and detachment. Perhaps, in those moments of quiet communion with the divine, he found the peace and clarity he had sought all his life.

For me, his absence is a void that no philosophy or practice can fill. He remains a part of me, not just in memories but in the lessons, he taught, the love he gave, and the resilience he embodied. Even in death, he continues to guide me, as though whispering through the silence, urging me to find my own path to acceptance.

Memories of him run vividly in my mind, encapsulated by the following verses.

HIM:

Glasses slipping down his nose,
A Gold Flake cigarette in repose,
In crinkled dhoti, silk Panjabi,
Kashmiri shawl, a sight to see—
The essence of a Bengali gent
A presence both refined and spent

Picky with tea, he sipped with grace
From gold-rimmed cups, in his own space
From politics to football, he'd switch with ease
Debating Netaji while sipping his tea
A walking encyclopaedia, wisdom in flow
With poetry and literature, his knowledge did grow

Humility defined him, as a true 'Bhadrolok'
At ease in crowds, a masterful cloak
A Bengali among Sahebs ,
a Saheb amongst his kin,
Such a breed of Bengali is rarely seen.

Bhadrolok- Bengali Gentleman
Saheb- Englishmen

The guilt of not being there for him during his final years weighs heavily on my heart. Watching Ma's transformation from a married woman to a widow was nothing short of devastating. The vibrant vermilion streak in her hair, once a symbol of life and love, disappeared, leaving behind a void that mirrored her new reality. In an instant, her world was turned upside down—her lively, non-vegetarian lifestyle was replaced by rigid traditions that dictated she embrace vegetarianism and overhaul her wardrobe to reflect her widowhood.

Ma, once a vibrant hibiscus red, transformed into a white dove, her head bowed in quiet grief. We, her children, were pained to see her without the '*sindur*' (vermilion) in her parting and her hands naked, without the bangles, associated with widowhood. She looked so helpless. I remember gently slipping the red and white bangles off her wrist. The vibrant red in her hair parting faded with each hair wash, replaced with a starkness, an unsettling contrast, that stung the eyes for many days.

Seeing the silent tears glisten on her serene face was unbearable. It was not just her loss—it was ours too. Yet, the traditions seemed more intent on stripping her of identity than offering solace. We siblings knew this had to change. Together, we resolved to challenge the conventions that only deepened her grief, even as Ma protested, reluctant to break away from what she believed was her duty.

It wasn't easy—it felt like a war of the Titans, but in the end, we prevailed. We allowed her to mourn on her terms, free from the weight of outdated rituals. *Breaking from tradition wasn't just about defying norms; it was about reclaiming her dignity and humanity in the face of loss.*

Timeless Traditions

Ma's transformation brings forth a flood of memories, taking me back to the Thursday rituals of my childhood, steeped in the sacred atmosphere of our home. Each Thursday was a celebration of Goddess Lakshmi, the revered goddess of wealth and prosperity. The day would begin with the resonant sound of the conch shell, its echo spreading throughout the house like a call to the divine. The fragrant wafts of incense would fill the air, enveloping us in a warm embrace of devotion, while the melodic chants of the *Lakshmi Path* (sacred hymn) stirred our hearts as day gracefully faded into dusk.

But the true spectacle lay in the preparations of the married women, especially Ma, who transformed into the resplendent Devi of the house. Adorned in her finest saree, she radiated a glow that was both beautiful and sacred. The air was filled with anticipation, laughter and the clinking of utensils as she prepared traditional sweets and offerings, each dish infused with love and devotion.

The spirit of the rituals was palpable—a tapestry of colours, scents and sounds that wove our family together in shared devotion. It was a time when our home felt alive with blessings, where every detail—every flower, every fruit—held significance, embodying our hopes and gratitude. These Thursday evenings were more than rituals; they were a celebration of our heritage, a moment to connect with the divine and with one another, a vibrant reminder of the richness of our culture and the bonds that held us together.

It all began with the mandatory hair wash using '*ritha*' (Indian soapberry), a ritual that Ma and her friends followed with unwavering faith. In those days, despite the allure of newly available shampoos, the old ways prevailed. Brands like 'Halo' and 'Palmolive', which promised convenience, remained untouched, gathering dust on the shelves. Instead, Ma and her circle swore by traditional remedies passed down through generations.

After washing her hair, Ma would settle on the open veranda, basking in the sun's warmth. There were no blow dryers then—only the natural drying power of the sun's rays and the gentle rustling of leaves in the breeze. The sunlight, filtered through the trees, cast a soft, golden glow that seemed to nourish both her hair and her spirit. In these quiet moments, with her tresses drying slowly, she felt deeply connected to nature and the wisdom of age-old practices.

At precisely 4 PM, '*Napith Bou*', the pedicurist, would arrive with her cloth bag, filled with tools for the weekly pampering ritual. I would watch in awe as she unpacked her treasures: a black pumice stone, a sharp hooked knife, a brass bowl with elegantly curved edges, and a bottle of '*alta*' (the deep red dye made from betel leaves), for decorating the feet. Ma would sit with her feet elevated on a wooden '*peeray*' (platform), her expression a mix of relaxation and anticipation.

Napith Bou would begin by soaping Ma's feet, rinsing them with warm water, and gently scrubbing them with the pumice stone to remove dry skin. With practised precision, *Bou* would wield the hooked knife, trimming overgrown nails and correcting any ingrown ones. A bottle of good old *Dettol* stood nearby, a silent guardian against mishaps.

As *Bou* worked, she would gossip, sharing snippets of news from her visits to other homes. I often leaned in, eager to catch the latest stories. The '*alta*' in the brass bowl looked like unset strawberry Jello. With a flourish, *Bou* would dip her thumb into it, painting intricate designs on Ma's feet—paisleys, hibiscus flowers, and other motifs reflecting the mood of the day. Once the feet were dry, *Bou* would turn her attention to Ma's hands, following the same meticulous care and decoration.

When her work was done, *Napith Bou,* graciously accepted the offer of a glass of chilled water from the '*suraï*' (earthen vessel) and a handful of '*batashaa*' (jaggery sweets). Her fee was a modest four annas (25 paise in existing currency), a small price for the luxury of her skilled touch. She left humming a tune under her breath, ready to entertain the next family with stories of her day.

Hair grooming was equally elaborate. Ma would spend what felt like an eternity in front of the mirror, applying oil with care and creating a perfect middle parting. A small '*gamcha*' (muslin towel) fashioned into a hair band would be knotted under her chin, while she coaxed her hair into delicate shapes, with wavy strands framing her face. A gold comb nestled in her bun, and with a thick smear of vermilion in her parting and a round *bindi*—the third eye—placed lovingly on her forehead, she transformed into the vision of a Bengali bride. She looked resplendent in her red-bordered saree, house keys thrown over her shoulder and the red, white and gold bangles adorning her hands. She embodied Goddess *Lakshmi* herself, ready to begin the Thursday puja rituals—dicing fruits into neat cubes, arranging them on gleaming bronze plates alongside homemade sweets, all while chanting the '*Lakshmi Path*' (holy chant) to invoke the goddess's presence. This ritual continued unchanged until the day she lost Baba.

Yet, she moved forward, bottling her grief for our sake. The pujas continued, but the Thursday rituals were lost. The grace with which she conducted herself through both joy and sorrow was evident in every aspect of her life. Hailing from a family of wealthy aristocrats, her marriage was arranged in a manner befitting her lineage—not through a matrimonial ad, but by the *Ghatak* (matchmaker), who carefully selected her for Baba. Baba often shared humorous tales of his first visit to her ancestral home in *Kashipur,* formerly what was part of East Bengal. He had been invited by her father, a third-generation *zamindar* (land owner), for their introductory meeting. Baba would recount his journey in a bullock cart, the women of Ma's family adorned in gold, greeting him with the blowing of the conch shells echoing in the air, and lavish meals served in engraved brassware. He also spoke of hunting partridges with the younger members of Ma's family. The image of my parents meeting for the first time, with Baba agreeing to the proposal without hesitation, paints a vivid picture of a different era.

Though Ma's family lost their home, land, and considerable wealth after the partition of Bengal, the richness of their traditions and memories endured, leaving a legacy that would forever shape our lives.

Traditions are the lifeblood of a culture, shaping its identity and keeping its history alive through generations. They are the rituals, practices and beliefs passed down from one era to the next, offering a sense of continuity and belonging. What's fascinating, however, is how some traditions manage to evolve alongside rapid technological advancements, running parallel to progress and adapting without losing their essence. These traditions, deeply rooted in culture, become the thread that ties the old with the new, blending the wisdom of the past with the possibilities of the future. It's heartening that many of these old traditions continue to exist, passed on from generation to generation.

CHAPTER SEVEN

New Beginnings 1991 onwards

Packing memories, joy, and tears
I face the pull of new frontiers
What if I stumble, and miss the past?
Yet growth calls, a spark that lasts
Life's a mosaic, old and new
Each piece adds colour, texture and hue
Though doubt may rise, my spirit will soar
In the journey, I'll find more.

New beginnings can be both exhilarating and daunting. The prospect of leaving the familiar—can stir up a mix of excitement and fear. On one hand, there's the thrill of possibility, the chance to explore new opportunities, and the growth potential. On the other hand, the unknown can be intimidating. Uncertainty looms large in the mind about losing connections, comfort, or the security of what we know. Add to that the fear of failure or not fitting into a new environment. There's also the anxiety of starting over, questioning whether I would have the resilience to navigate uncharted waters.

Moving to another city had its share of all the above. Would the girls miss their old school and friends? Would I reconcile to being homebound after twenty-odd years of a 9 to 5 job? Would that impact my mental health and by extension affect my relationship with others?

My initial apprehensions were totally unfounded. As we settled into our new environment, it felt as if we had slipped into a glove—perfectly moulded to our needs and desires. The contrast with our previous life was striking. We had moved from the frenetic pace of a bustling metro to a serene haven aptly named "Pensioner's Paradise", where life moved on the slow lane.

At first, I feared the change would be overwhelming. The shift from the hot, humid climate, we were accustomed to, brought a wave of uncertainty. What if the different climate didn't suit us? I wondered if I would miss the vibrant energy of city life. However, the moment we arrived in Bangalore, appropriately carrying the tagline, "Air-conditioned City," I realized how much I had longed for the gentle breeze that eliminated the need for fans year-round. Each step along the tree-lined avenues was like stepping into a postcard; the lush greenery and expansive lung spaces were a feast for the senses—cool and soothing, an antidote to my earlier anxiety.

As we drove through the tranquil streets, I felt my worries about navigating this new terrain dissipate. Gone were the days of honking horns and chaotic traffic jams. Here, driving was a delightful experience, marked by the quiet hum of our car gliding smoothly along wide roads, surrounded by nature instead of concrete. The stillness was refreshing, almost surreal compared to the constant noise we had left behind.

One of my biggest concerns had been how we would manage our daughters' school runs in this unfamiliar place. I dreaded the thought of navigating routes and finding reliable transportation. To my delight, the reality was far from my fears. The convenience of a mere ten-minute walk to school was not only a relief but also an opportunity. Our daughters quickly fell into a routine, joining a vibrant gang of students from our apartment complex. Initially, we drove them for those first few years, still wary of letting them venture out on their own. When they graduated to walking down with others, I felt a twinge of hesitation—would they be safe? Would they adapt? Thankfully, with each passing day, we watched them grow more confident, until finally, we were able to encourage them to walk alongside their friends.

This gradual transition transformed our apprehensions into a sense of community and connection. What once felt daunting became a source of joy and pride. The worries I had held onto began to fade, replaced by a profound appreciation for our new life. With every step we took in this peaceful paradise, I found solace in the fact that we had truly embraced a new chapter, one that exceeded all my expectations.

Moving into a gated apartment complex after decades of living in stand-alone homes, was a new experience. Neighbours, eager to help us feel comfortable in their cosmopolitan community, extended their support in countless ways—helping us find domestic staff, and recommending doctors, pharmacies, and essential services. This felt like a warm extension of the familiarity we had left behind, with only minor differences. Soon enough, we began to settle in and feel a sense of belonging.

Once the initial settling process was complete, I turned my focus to finding gainful employment that aligned with my experience. Opportunities abounded, and I honed in on companies that had relocated from Calcutta, hoping the work culture would mirror what I was accustomed to. To my dismay, it was nothing like what I had anticipated. The reality was a far cry from my expectations, which had been set high for a city still in its nascent stages of growth.

After two years of struggling with a formerly Calcutta-based company, I ultimately decided to hang up my boots for compelling reasons. I felt I was underperforming, though I couldn't fully grasp why at the time, till realisation hit me slowly, like a creeping shadow. I began to notice that I was speaking louder than usual, straining to hear conversations on the phone, and needing to turn up the volume on the Dictaphone to take down notes and instructions. I found myself repeatedly asking people to repeat themselves, a simple request that felt increasingly humiliating. Each incident chipped away at my self-esteem, igniting fears of isolation and rejection. It was difficult to face the possibility that I might be suffering from hearing loss—something I had desperately tried to deny.

Multiple visits to audiologists confirmed my worst fears: I was indeed facing a genetic predisposition to hearing loss, inherited from my mother's side. She had begun losing her hearing in her late fifties, just like her father. The knowledge that this disorder had chosen me among all my siblings felt like a cruel twist of fate. Accepting this diagnosis in my early forties was overwhelming, filling me with a sense of shame and fear of the future. I worried about how my family and colleagues would perceive me, how my career might be impacted, and whether I would ever truly belong again.

After careful deliberation and at my husband's urging, I made up my mind to quit the workforce. I became a full-time mom to the family's delight. The adjustment process was swift; I took over the usual household chores and ran outside errands, relieving my husband of many shared responsibilities. While I embraced my new role, I couldn't shake off the nagging anxiety that accompanied my diagnosis and the shadow of my hearing loss loomed large, a constant reminder of my struggle for normalcy in a world that suddenly felt more isolating than before.

That was when I dived into cooking, something I had no real experience with, but it soon became my refuge, a way to channel my anxiety and find a sense of normalcy amidst the changes in my life, especially as I navigated the challenges of my hearing loss. The kitchen became my sanctuary. The rhythmic clatter of pots and pans served as a comforting soundtrack that drowned out my worries. As I immersed myself in the process, focusing on textures, aromas, and flavours, I found relief from the uncertainties that often clouded my thoughts.

Cooking, over time, transformed into a meditative practice. Chopping vegetables, stirring sauces, and watching ingredients evolve under heat became moments of peace. Each step required my full attention, pulling me away from my anxious mind. The repetitive motions of cooking were soothing, creating a flow that calmed my nerves and grounded me in the present. What had once been a task I avoided, now felt like a source of stability.

I also discovered cooking as a creative outlet—a way to express myself without the pressures of external expectations. Experimenting with new recipes helped me reclaim a sense of well-being. It was no longer about simply feeding my family, but about creating something beautiful and delicious. I involved my daughters in the process, turning them into enthusiastic tasters. Together, we explored flavours and textures, building memories while strengthening our bond. Each meal became an opportunity to provide warmth and comfort, a reminder that I was still deeply connected to the vibrant world around me despite my challenges.

As I honed my culinary skills, I began to see cooking as a reflection of my personal growth. Just like I was learning to adapt to my hearing loss, I learned to embrace change and experimentation in the kitchen. Challenges became growth opportunities—whether it was mastering a new cooking technique or adapting recipes to fit our dietary needs. Each success, no matter how small, built my confidence and resilience.

The rewards of my newfound passion were tangible. The tiffin boxes I packed for my daughters earned praise from their friends. Coin pizzas, cabbage rolls, and minced cutlets became repeat requests, and the joy of seeing them enjoy my creations was incredibly fulfilling. Ma's request for hot, fluffy '*phulkas*' (Indian flatbread) with melting butter was another victory. It was a simple thing, but it lifted my spirits. Finally, the rolling pin and I had become friends, and I marvelled at how far I had come—from not knowing how to cook to dishing out gourmet meals that brought smiles and satisfaction to my family. Cooking not only nourished our bodies but also helped nourish my soul.

At this juncture, buoyed by my husband's support, I returned to the classroom and resumed pursuing an online MBA degree from IGNOU. Instead of supervising the girl's studies, I joined them in completing our homework together—working through assignments side by side. This sense of fulfilment helped to overshadow the disappointment I felt at being labelled "handicapped" and the shame I experienced about wearing hearing aids. Returning to my studies provided a new perspective. It became a space where I could focus on my capabilities rather than my limitations. Each assignment completed, felt like a small victory, a step toward reclaiming my identity, and I found myself gradually shedding the weight of shame and embracing a journey of growth and self-acceptance. I owe a big deal to hubby for his guidance and encouragement to see me through this journey, which took two years to complete successfully.

On the downside, I grew reluctant to attend office parties and social gatherings, my anxiety about my hearing loss casting a long shadow over my confidence. When attending events became unavoidable, I would hesitate to engage in conversation, listening rather than talking. It was exhausting—both physically and emotionally. The effort to hide my hearing aids added a layer of tension to situations that should have been enjoyable.

However, embracing these fears turned out to be a powerful part of my journey. Acknowledging them helped me understand what I was leaving behind and why it mattered, motivating me to prepare, learn, and adapt. In the unfamiliar, I discovered strengths I didn't know I could tap into. And while the transition was fraught with challenges, it was also the starting point where transformation happened.

Cut to the present and on a lighter vein: what once felt like a disadvantage has turned into a quirky superpower exclusive to those of us with hearing loss. Seriously, it's like having an on-demand noise-cancellation feature! You know that moment when you're finally settling in for a peaceful evening, and suddenly the neighbours decide it's the perfect time for an all-night dance party? Well, I just flick the switch and—voila! —it's like someone hit the mute button on the chaos.

And the best part? While everyone else is tossing and turning, wide awake from barking dogs or late-night shenanigans, I'm snoozing like a baby. It's like having a secret shield against the world's noise. One flick of a switch, and I'm transported to my serene oasis, unapologetically enjoying my peaceful sleep. Who knew a little hearing loss could bring such an unexpected perk?

Empty Nest

I take the blame for stalling it for three years for the older one. She had earned a full scholarship to pursue graduate studies in the USA right after high school. My heart swelled with pride, but my mind was filled with doubt and worry. As a mother, my protective instincts kicked in full force. Wasn't she still too young to venture out on her own in a foreign country? The thought of her getting sick, feeling lonely, or falling in with the wrong crowd rushed through my mind like a runaway train.

We went back and forth, her youthful enthusiasm clashing with my fears. In the end, I made a promise to her: I wouldn't stand in her way once she turned twenty-one—once she was older, more mature, and perhaps a little less reliant on me. But even as I said it, I knew that my decision came with a heavy cost. It felt like I was shattering her dreams, all in the name of trying to protect her and that realization tore at my heart. It was a choice I had to make, but it broke me to know that in protecting her, I was, in some way, breaking her too.

She didn't say much after that, but I could see the disappointment in her eyes, the unspoken pain. I had delayed her future, and in the process, I had made her question whether I truly believed in her. That hurt more than I cared to admit.

Three years later she completed her graduate studies, securing another fully paid scholarship for her PhD in the USA. This time, however, I stood on the sidelines with no roadblocks. I felt a bittersweet mix of pride and sorrow as I packed her bags, knowing she was ready to take on the world. Yet, with each item I folded, I could feel the empty nest looming.

As I waved goodbye at the airport, I felt a profound sense of loss wash over me. My firstborn was stepping out into the world, full of confidence and aspirations, while I was left behind, grappling with her absence. The house that once bustled with her laughter and energy suddenly felt hollow. The walls seemed to close in, and the familiar routines became reminders of her absence.

In the weeks that followed her departure, I found myself colliding with the emptiness of an empty nest. I missed her chatter, her lively presence at the dining table, the spontaneous outings, and the small moments that had strengthened our bond. I often wondered if she was eating well or feeling lonely in her new surroundings. The concerns that had once seemed manageable now felt magnified by the miles between us.

Then, just over a year later, the attacks on the Twin Towers on September 11, 2001, plunged us into a new wave of anxiety. Even though we knew she was far from the site of the tragedy, the uncertainty and fear were overwhelming. Every hour, we called just to hear her voice, seeking reassurance that she was safe. Each call offered momentary relief, yet the persistent worry lingered, a constant reminder of how distance could amplify our deepest fears.

There was still some comfort in the knowledge that our nest was only half-empty. The younger one was like the Rock of Gibraltar, filling the void left by her sister in more ways than one. Her infectious joie de vivre brought a new energy into our home, brightening our days and reminding us of the joy that still lingered within our family. However, this solace was short-lived. Within a year, she left to pursue her engineering studies, in a location far away from home which required her to stay on campus. The next four years became a tragicomic dance of having her around and then letting her go. We cherished the weekends and vacations when she would return home, filling our lives with laughter and warmth, even if only for a little while.

In 2007 she left for the USA to pursue an MBA. With her departure, the emptiness in our home became palpable, transforming our half-empty nest into one that felt achingly hollow. It was as if the glass, which had once felt half-full with her vibrant energy, now stood completely empty.

Yet, I tried to embrace the half-empty glass theory. Instead of focusing on what I had lost, I reminded myself of the precious memories we had created and the incredible women they were becoming. Though they were far away, their spirits lived on in our home, and I found comfort in knowing that their journeys were just beginning.

I tried to distract myself—filling my days with activities, reconnecting with friends, and even picking up new hobbies. Yet, no matter how busy I kept myself, there was a gnawing feeling of emptiness, that I couldn't shake off. The silence was deafening and the house felt like a museum of memories, each corner echoing their absence.

But in the quiet moments, I also realized that this was part of their journey. My heart ached, yes, but it also swelled with pride. They were out there, conquering challenges, growing into the remarkable women I always knew they could be. As I navigated this new chapter, I learned to embrace the silence, understanding that my role as a mother would evolve, even if it meant letting go. After all, love doesn't diminish with distance; it simply transforms.

Mother-daughter time

This phase of my life began in 2002 when my daughters left home to pursue higher studies. With newfound time on my hands, I chose to dedicate myself to my ageing mother. It felt like an opportunity to give back for all the moments she had sacrificed while raising us. As I reflected, I realized that during all those years when Baba would take us out for movies, shopping, and Sunday breakfasts at Flury's, Ma often chose not to join us. At the time, I thought it was her personal choice. But looking back, I began to wonder: Was she disinterested or deliberately avoided these outings? Perhaps to keep the expenses down, sacrificing her own pleasure for ours. As I grew older, I started to sense the quiet sacrifices she had made.

I wanted to make up for all the fun she had missed, so I established a weekly routine: every Friday, we would go out for the matinee show, catching the latest Bollywood releases. The joy on her face as we settled into our seats, with bags of popcorn and Coke in hand, revealed how much she cherished these simple pleasures. It became clear to me that, in her quiet way, she had given up so much for the sake of our happiness. These small outings—laughing together in the dim light of the theatre—were moments that I treasured deeply.

This time together allowed me to take her on pilgrimages and short vacations whenever my husband travelled for work. One of the most unforgettable trips was to Shirdi, where I witnessed her serene contentment standing before the Saint. I vividly remember the silent tears streaming down her cheeks during the early morning *darshans*, (viewing of the Saint) her lips moving in heartfelt prayer. It soon became an annual tradition. Each visit was a testament to her unwavering faith, and we often stayed for several *darshans* before catching the train back home. Those moments, filled with peace and devotion, remain etched in my memory.

Although a devout Hindu of Brahmin caste, she was never confined by rigidity in her beliefs. Her faith was expansive, transcending the boundaries of her religious upbringing. She accompanied me to the Infant Jesus Church on Thursdays, where we prayed and lit candles together. Under her pillow, pictures of Lord Krishna, Shirdi Baba, and Infant Jesus lay side by side—a profound testament to her unwavering embrace of the divine in all its forms. That spirit of acceptance and devotion defined her, staying with her until the very end.

The last trip was in 2004, just two years before she passed away in 2006 at the age of eighty-four. Before leaving for his overseas trip, my husband had booked a stay for us at a jungle resort on the Kabini River. Despite the long, bumpy drive, her spirit remained unshaken. At the resort, she surprised everyone by enthusiastically participating in all the activities, her joy infectious to both guests and staff. We took a coracle ride on the river, her laughter ringing out as the boat bobbed on the water. We sat on the riverbank for hours, fishing for the elusive '*Humpback Mahseer* (fish found in the river Cauvery, and on the list of endangered species), exchanging stories and enjoying each other's company.

At eighty-two, she was reclaiming the joy she had put aside for so long. Watching her embrace these moments of freedom and excitement filled my heart with pride. It was as though, in those last few years, she was making up for all the things she had postponed. She was a trouper in every sense.

Each outing with her deepened my appreciation for her sacrifices. It made me realize just how much she had given up, not out of obligation, but from a deep sense of love and duty. The bond we forged during these years became a sanctuary for both of us—a space where love, laughter, and memories intertwined. Looking back, I am filled with an overwhelming sense of gratitude for the woman who had given so much of herself, not only to raise us but to ensure we had the best of everything.

And without any warning, her health began deteriorating in 2005, a year that marked a profound shift in our lives. Ma, a healthy woman full of vitality, suddenly began to change in ways we couldn't comprehend. Her usual warmth and positivity, which had been her hallmark, dimmed into a quiet confusion. She, who had always relished our post-dinner ice cream outings, now resisted, her appetite waning, leaving us concerned.

"Ma, are you feeling, okay?" I would ask, trying to gauge her mood.

"I'm fine, dear," she'd reply, though the sparkle in her eyes had dulled.

Despite her reassurances, I felt a growing unease. Doctors couldn't find anything physically wrong. Their dismissals—phrases like "old-age eccentricities"—stung. It was as if they were trivializing her struggles.

"Ma, let's go to the temple," I suggested one evening, hoping to reignite some joy. Her response "I'm not up to it" had me worried. Her usual routine faltered with her once-dedicated prayer times shrinking, a rare admission of her discomfort. It was clear that something deeper was amiss. I watched helplessly as her spirit seemed to slip away. Then one day, I found her at the temple in her room, her hands clasped in fervent prayer, her voice barely above a whisper. "Please, God... make me well." It was a painful plea that echoed through my heart, a desperate call for help from a woman who had always been my rock. Repeated visits to doctors and diagnostic examinations, revealed nothing of concern.

The decision to move her to Calcutta for a change of scenery came with the hope that familiar surroundings would rejuvenate her spirit. Calcutta was where her memories thrived, the city buzzing with voices she recognized, the language she understood better than any other language. I felt the weight of her fragility when leaving her in Calcutta.

“Don’t worry, I’ll be fine,” she assured, but her eyes told a different story.

By June 2006, when she returned, the transformation was shocking. The vibrant woman I knew had been reduced to a shadow. The mental decline was heartbreaking. I remember sitting beside her one evening, her frail hand in mine.

“Ma, can you hear me?” I whispered, my voice trembling.

“Of course, dear,” she replied, though her gaze was distant, lost in a fog I couldn’t penetrate.

Then came the stroke. Three days in the ICU felt like an eternity. I watched her, once so strong, now utterly vulnerable. The sight of her with a nasogastric tube broke something inside me. It was a cruel twist of fate, the most courageous woman I knew was reduced to someone so fragile.

When the nurse we hired failed to provide the care she needed, resulting in painful bedsores, my heart sank.

“What are we going to do?” I asked my husband and younger one, desperation creeping into my voice.

“We need to consider professional help,” one of them suggested.

With the doctor’s stern yet compassionate advice, we faced an agonizing decision. “She can either suffer at home or be moved to a hospice where she can receive proper care,” he explained, the gravity of the situation weighing heavily on us. “I promise she will return home."

My heart shattered at the thought. "But what if she needs us?" I protested, tears blurring my vision.

"Think of her suffering, at home without necessary medical tools. "It's about what's best for her now", the hospice in-charge threw in my face.

Reluctantly, I agreed. We chose to send her away, believing it would be for the best. Yet as we drove her to the hospice, a deep sense of dread enveloped me.

"Ma, we'll visit every day," I promised, though I couldn't shake the feeling that I was abandoning her.

I remember the last time I saw her. She lay there, surrounded by unfamiliar faces, her once-bright spirit dimmed. I held her hand tightly. "I love you, Ma. I will take you home soon", I whispered, hoping she could hear me through the haze. The attending doctor had assured me they would do their best to get her on her feet. And so, I believed, clutching onto that thought, in the hope of having her back with us for many more years.

Ten days of her stay and then I received the news that would haunt me forever—she passed away alone, in a place where she felt no comfort. The guilt of not being there during her last moments consumed me.

If I could change one thing in my life, it would be that decision to send her away. I wish I could have held her hand, played her favourite hymns, and soothed her as she made her final journey.

"Why didn't I fight harder?" I often ask myself, wrestling with the sorrow of that choice. Her absence is a void that echoes the unfulfilled promise of love and care I had envisaged for her. I always carry this weight with me, a reminder of the fragility of life and the profound pain of saying goodbye.

Performing the last rites was an excruciating experience—one we were unprepared for. Without the guidance or support of family or extended relatives, it was just my husband, our younger one, and me, struggling to navigate the intricate Hindu rituals that felt overwhelming in their unfamiliarity.

The memory of her body reduced to ashes with the strike of a match is seared into my mind. The moment her body slid into the furnace and ignited instantly was devastating—a stark, irreversible finality that haunts me still.

I can still feel the weight of the urn in my hands as I carried her ashes, my voice trembling as I chanted the *Gayatri Mantra* (Hindu chant). Mid-stream at the Sangam, I found myself prolonging the immersion, as if delaying it could somehow reverse the inevitable and bring her back. The ache of letting go was unbearable, a pain etched into my soul forever.

In the aftermath, our world shattered. The grief was overwhelming, beyond anything we could comprehend. My husband, the younger one, and I clung to each other for comfort, spending sleepless nights replaying the events that led to her passing. Entering her bedroom felt like walking on glass shards—each step a reminder of our loss. This unbearable reality stretched on for months.

I had never truly understood that grief comes in waves until now. Each wave crashed over me unexpectedly, pulling me under with a force that left me gasping. Some days were manageable; I could breathe through the memories, allowing them to wash over me like gentle rain. On other days, the tide would rise, dragging me into an abyss of sorrow and making me question how we could move forward without her.

Time blurred into a haze, days blending into each other. Each morning felt like waking up to an echo, a reminder of her absence in the smallest rituals—her favourite tea left untouched, her chair at the table forever empty. Friends reached out, some offering kind words, others unsure of how to navigate our grief, their silence heavy and awkward.

I began to realize that grief isn't a linear journey; it spirals back to the same painful memories, often offering a different perspective. I learned to embrace those waves of emotion, allowing them to wash over me while accepting the depth of my loss. Though the pain still lingers, it has started to intertwine with gratitude for the time we shared, the lessons she imparted, and the enduring love that surrounds us.

Ma's departure left a gaping hole in my life—a profound loss that I still struggle to come to terms with. I often find myself wishing she were still here, marvelling at her great-grandchildren and perhaps chuckling at the sight of me—a grey-haired septuagenarian, with stooped shoulders, and fingers flying on the keyboard to chronicle her life journey.

And I thought with time,
my memory of her
would hit 'Escape'
The 'Backspace' of Life
would erase the pain
And 'Control'would be restored.
I was so, wrong

She is still there,
saved in my 'Cloud'
A file I open and revisit endlessly,
reliving the moments

We shared on this earth

Pinned like a favourite tab,
present in every 'Shift'
and 'Enter'of my life
Now my Home Key

Mothers have a curious, almost magical knack for freezing their children in time. For her, I was forever thirsty. Why? Because mothers seem to cling to the child nestled within the adult we've become, no matter how many birthdays we pile on. It's like they're stuck in a time loop, squinting at us through the rose-tinted lens of their memories. This peculiar talent can be both endearing and exasperating—making us feel perpetually young while simultaneously reducing us to toddlers, incapable of tying our own shoelaces. But if I'm honest, I secretly loved it. Who wouldn't enjoy feeling youthful, even as the crow's feet tell a different story?

Wishing for her presence today is like trying to hug a cloud—beautifully impossible yet irresistibly tempting. It's human nature, isn't it? To yearn for the unattainable—immortality, perfect love, a metabolism that defies cake. These improbable desires aren't just wishful thinking; they're proof of our capacity to dream big and love deeply, even when reality insists on playing party pooper.

In chasing what we can't have and longing for moments we can't relive, we uncover our most human qualities: vulnerability and hope. These twin threads weave the fabric of life—fragile yet resilient, bittersweet but meaningful. After all, what's life without a little yearning?

CHAPTER EIGHT

The vacuum

In shadows deep where memories dwell
A heart once full now holds a shell
Each tear a tribute, each sigh a song
In the echoes of love, we learn to be strong

The silence in our home became deafening, filled with memories of Ma and the girls now far away. Ma's departure in 2006, and a year later with the younger one leaving for the USA—the loneliness I felt was profound and all-consuming. The silence felt like a thick fog, wrapping around me and refusing to lift. Each room echoed with memories—laughter in the kitchen, the girls' voices singing off-key, Ma's gentle reminders to order fresh Puja flowers for her daily needs. The house that once buzzed with life became an empty shell. I would sit for hours in the living room, staring at the old photographs, tracing the outlines of our shared moments. It felt surreal; the world outside moved on, but I was stuck in a loop of grief and nostalgia.

For a long time, I resisted acknowledging my feelings, hoping that time would smooth the edges of my loneliness. But it only deepened, carving itself into my routine. I missed the small, mundane moments we used to share—the evening cups of tea, and drives around the city. I became a ghost in my own life, drifting through days without purpose or direction, caught in a cycle of longing and loss.

This isolation took a serious toll on my health. My husband, seeking to pull me from this morass, suggested we move to another city where he was setting up a multinational company. We hoped that a change of scenery would alleviate some of the sorrow. But despite two years of Allopathic, Ayurvedic, and Homeopathic treatments, my physical and mental health showed little improvement.

Overseas vacations and visits to the girls provided only temporary relief, leaving me feeling lost and disconnected. I struggled to recognize the person I had become. At fifty-five, reverting to my former self felt like climbing a steep mountain. I sought comfort in visiting religious places, hoping to find solace in spirituality.

Yet, the challenges of overcoming grief and loneliness were relentless. Each day felt like a battle against the weight of absence, as I grappled with the pain of loss while yearning for connection. In those quiet moments, I realized that healing would take time, and learning to live with the memories of love was a journey I had to embrace, one step at a time.

It took a long time to understand that adjusting to this new reality wasn't just about filling the silence; it was about learning to live with the echoes of those we love. The loneliness didn't fade; instead, it transformed. It became a part of me—a reminder of the love that once was and the memories that still lingered.

Unions

In 2010, when my younger daughter announced her intention to marry her senior from engineering college, I was caught in a rush of conflicting emotions. On one hand, there was the joy and excitement of planning a wedding, a momentous occasion that would bring an addition to our family and fill our home with celebration. On the other, there was the deep, underlying current of anxiety and emotional upheaval that had been my constant companion for the last few years.

It wasn't just the wedding itself—though that was a whirlwind in its own right, with endless shopping, booking venues, negotiating with caterers, and handling the thousands of little details that seemed to multiply by the day. It was more than that. It was the concern if we could pull it off without any hiccups.

As I immersed myself in the wedding preparations, something started to shift within me. Perhaps it was the sheer volume of activity—the constant need to make decisions, plan and ensure everything fell into place that forced me to engage with the world in a way I hadn't in a long time. There was no room to dwell in isolation or let my thoughts spiral inward; I had no choice but to focus on the present and the future we were building together.

The emotional shift was subtle, catalysed by the interplay of joy and grief. Planning her wedding meant holding two emotions at once:

the joy of seeing her embrace a new chapter in her life and the sorrow of knowing it marked a change in mine. She had always been my anchor, and now I had to learn to let go—just as she was learning to step into a life of independence and promise.

Yet, in that letting go, something began to heal. Organizing her celebration became a cathartic experience. It gave me purpose, a connection to something larger than myself, and a reason to celebrate life rather than simply endure it. As I poured myself into the preparations, the sadness that had weighed on me for so long slowly began to lift.

The love and excitement surrounding the wedding pulled me forward, inch by inch. Each dress fitting, each conversation with caterers and each decision about flowers or guest lists nudged me out of the fog of despair. It didn't happen in one dramatic moment but rather in countless small moments of joy that added up, reminding me that I had a place in this world and that life could still hold beauty and meaning. It was a joy with a sting in the tail—there were tears and moments of overwhelming emotion—but it was also a lightness, a realization that I could still feel deeply, still experience happiness.

Her wedding, as much as it was a joyous occasion, was also the final stage of a profound personal transformation for me. It marked the moment when my life, once defined by sorrow and isolation, slowly began to redefine itself through love, purpose, and the recognition that there was so much more ahead. I was no longer merely drifting, but choosing to move forward, for her, for myself, and for the new chapter that awaited us all.

The day of the wedding was a kaleidoscope of emotions—joy intertwined with a poignant ache in my heart. I revelled in the beauty of her happiness, yet I couldn't help but feel a twinge of sadness at the thought of her stepping into a new life. As I watched her, radiant in her wedding attire, I realized that this was not just a celebration of love, but a profound transition—a reminder of the delicate balance between joy and sorrow that defines a mother's heart.

It was a wedding to remember with our families (living in other cities) and friends, joining in for the three-day event filled with fun, food, and a learning experience embracing new customs and a brand-new extended family.

Indian weddings are a vibrant tapestry of colours, rituals, and emotions, each thread woven from the diverse cultures that inhabit the subcontinent. While the specifics may vary from region to region—be it the elaborate Punjabi celebrations, the graceful South Indian ceremonies, or the intricate Bengali customs—the essence remains strikingly similar: a joyous union of two families, a celebration of love, and the beginning of a new chapter. And at the heart of every wedding lies the concept of togetherness. The rituals may change, but the emotions remain universal.

In 2013, just three years later, the older one surprised us with the announcement of her engagement to a colleague from the university. Our joy knew no bounds as we welcomed another member into our growing family—this time an American, which meant planning an intercultural wedding in the USA.

The wedding was a beautiful fusion of traditions, but organizing it came with its challenges. The groom's mother, a meticulous planner, took charge, ensuring every detail was attended to while keeping me in the loop throughout the process. For six months, we communicated daily via email, sharing ideas and navigating the complexities of blending our Eastern customs with Western practices.

As we collaborated, our relationship blossomed from mere "moms" to the best of friends. We brainstormed ways to incorporate meaningful rituals from both cultures, discussing everything from the ceremony to the food. By the time the wedding day arrived, we had crafted a celebration that honoured both families, beautifully merging our traditions. The joy of acquiring a new friend through this experience was a gift I hadn't anticipated. Despite the miles between us, our friendship continues to thrive, a testament to the love that unites our families and the richness of our shared journey.

First-time grandparents

We had promised ourselves: "No asking, no pushing. We'll let them take their time, even if it means waiting an eternity." With no expectations, there was no anticipation. So, one cosy evening, wrapped in a blanket and immersed in a Netflix movie, the phone rang, jolting us from our cinematic escape. The ringtone—distinctly international—sent a rush of curiosity and nerves through us.

"Is it them?" I whispered, my heart racing as hubby picked up the receiver. "Put it on speaker!" I urged, my excitement bubbling just beneath the surface. As he pressed the button, the phone crackled to life, and we both leaned in, eager to hear what news awaited us.

The voice on the other end, tinged with a somewhat grim tone, sent a chill down my spine. "Can you both hear me?" she asked. Fear and anxiety spiralled in my mind. What could it be? My pulse quickened, and I exchanged a worried glance with hubby. Then, as if sensing our trepidation, her voice brightened and I felt my breath hitch. "I have news... You're going to be grandparents!"

For a moment, silence enveloped us, punctuated only by the sound of our hearts pounding in our ears. "Did we hear that right?" I mouthed to hubby, who looked equally stunned, his eyes wide with disbelief. The grim tone melted away into pure joy, and suddenly we were swept up in a whirlwind of conversation, laughter, and tears of happiness. “Are you serious?!” I exclaimed, my voice cracking with emotion.

“Yes! I’m pregnant!” she said, her excitement radiating through the phone. The babbling that ensued, transcending oceans and miles, felt like a symphony celebrating new beginnings.

“Oh my gosh! This is incredible!” I said, my heart soaring. Hubby grabbed my hand tightly, squeezing it as if to ground himself in this whirlwind of joy.

“I can’t believe it! We’re going to be grandparents!” he echoed, a beaming smile breaking across his face.

As the conversation flowed, we felt our lives shift, the weight of impending grandparenting crashing over us like a warm wave of sunshine. Ideas danced in our minds—what kind of grandparents would we be? What adventures awaited us?

“I guess we better start brushing up on grandparenting!” I laughed, and we both burst into joyous chatter, the anxiety of waiting washed away by the thrill of this new role. The world felt a little brighter and a little more vibrant and we knew, without a doubt, that we were ready for this beautiful adventure.

Travel plans to the U.S. commenced immediately, with booking the airline tickets closer to the expected delivery date. But the little one had other ideas, arriving thirteen days early. I’ll never forget the grandmotherly instincts kicking in the moment I picked her up from her mother’s lap, a mere eight days old. A beautiful girl, our first grandchild.

The joy of this new life brought our two families together in a way we never expected. For two whole weeks, we celebrated, passing the tiny bundle around like a precious trophy. We peered closely at her puckered face, playfully debating who she resembled. “She definitely has her mother’s nose!” I’d say, only to be countered with, “No way! That chin is all her father!” Eventually, we settled on a delightful mix of West and East, the merging of our two worlds.

Now, at ten years old, I often find myself reminiscing about those early days. I can still hear hubby softly singing her to sleep with the same Hindi lullabies he once sang to her mother. Tears well in my eyes as I find myself caught between the present and the past, grateful for those fleeting moments we shared right after her birth.

On the day of departure, our hearts felt heavy with the thought of leaving her behind. I hugged our daughter and son-in-law tightly, respecting their wishes to parent their child without our interference during her maternity leave. Yet, as I walked out the door, the tears flowed freely, unsure when next we would see her. Returning home felt surreal. Our Sunday calls took on new significance, transforming into a lifeline that connected us across the miles. Each week, we eagerly awaited the updates, clinging to every word about her growth and milestones. I longed to hear about her progress and the little quirks that made her uniquely her. Though the distance was hard, it was in those calls that I felt the warmth of our bond.

The real journey into grandparenting began in April 2015, marked by an agreement between two moms regarding the babysitting schedule after my daughter returned to work. This arrangement would last until our grandchild was ready for the daycare centre they had chosen through the university facility. Whoopee! The handover from one grandmother to another was a tear-jerking moment, as one grandmother left empty-handed while the other embraced her seven-month-old grandchild with outstretched arms, filled with a mix of nervousness and excitement.

In those early days, I cherished every moment—feeding, changing diapers, watching her sleep, and catching the fleeting expressions that danced across her tiny face. Her smile upon waking felt like a sunrise, illuminating my heart. Tasks I thought were long behind me suddenly came rushing back, each one executed with a newfound sense of purpose and joy. My husband joined me a month later, which introduced a new dynamic: sharing precious time for joint grandparenting.

After six weeks, we found ourselves pondering the impending transition from home to daycare. How would this shift affect her? The thought of others feeding and putting her to sleep made us feel uneasy.

This new approach—placing children in daycare—was becoming the norm across both continents, especially within nuclear families, where grandparents often lived far away. While we got to understand that daycare centres provide structured environments and socialization opportunities, we felt that they would lack the warmth and individualized attention that grandparents can offer. But then the world was evolving. And we needed to fit into this new order of change, knowing that was best for our grandchild.

While ruminating over the loss of not hearing our granddaughter's delightful cries and infectious laughter and witnessing her charming little tantrums, a wave of joyous news swept in: our younger daughter was pregnant! Another grandchild was on the way, just six months later. This time, we wouldn't have to traverse the seven seas to live our new roles.

In December 2015, we welcomed our second grandchild—our first grandson! After raising a household full of girls and navigating the world of all things pink, I was over the moon to dive into the new adventure of grandparenting with a little boy. But let's just say, I was 'a little' unprepared. Apparently, there's an art to dodging the unexpected spray when changing diapers that I had yet to master.

After a few surprise "incidents," I was questioning whether I was cut out for this. Luckily, my daughter, a seasoned pro by then, graciously shared her hard-earned wisdom—though I suspect she enjoyed watching me fumble through the learning curve!

Our babysitting schedule with our grandson was a thrilling five days a week. Each Sunday evening, we'd pile into the car with our suitcases, practically buzzing with anticipation as we headed to our daughter's home. The week flew by in a blur of giggles, diaper changes, and the inevitable heart-tugging moment when we had to say goodbye every Friday. Those departures became a little tougher each time, transforming from cheerful waves to stealthy exits. If we weren't quiet enough, we'd risk a full-blown meltdown!

Our little guy quickly became Grandpa's shadow, sticking to him like a tiny, affectionate storm cloud. The moment he learned to crawl, he claimed Grandpa's lap as his throne, hijacked his laptop, and even turned that heavy wristwatch of Grandpa's into a toy. Honestly, it was hard to tell who was spoiling whom! Watching their bond grow was pure magic—it filled my heart with a warmth and nostalgia I hadn't expected. It reminded me of a line from 'The Sound of Music': "But somewhere in my youth or childhood, I must have done something good." This joy, this connection, felt like a beautiful reward for all those years of love and care we had put into raising our family. Each week brought a delightful mix of chaos and laughter and I couldn't help but smile at how, after all these years, I was once again a rookie in the grandparenting game. It was an adventure I hadn't known I needed and one I'd never want to miss.

Recalling his second birthday party brings a mix of embarrassment and joy. Dressed like a mini boardroom executive in a suit and bow tie, he clung tightly to his grandpa, preventing other family members and guests from interacting with him. We quickly retreated to give others a chance to connect, feeling both amused and protective.

When his parents decided to return to work onsite after a year of remote work, we reluctantly agreed to their choice to enrol him in daycare, marking the end of our regular babysitting days. Yet weekends and holidays became a treasure trove of shared moments, filled with laughter and play. Joining the 'Grandparents Day' program at the daycare was a highlight, with his eyes lighting up when he saw his grandpa. Those moments of connection filled our hearts with a joy we hadn't anticipated.

Recognizing the profound happiness our grandson brought us; we made a significant decision: to move closer. With our daughter and son-in-law's support, we transitioned from a forty-minute drive to just ten minutes. By the time he turned three in 2017, we were settled into our new home, excited about the possibilities ahead.

This proximity enriched our lives in ways we hadn't imagined. It created a support system that allowed us to be actively involved in his growth—sharing spontaneous playdates, attending his activities, and simply enjoying togetherness moments.

That's when we realized that even the strictest parents often transform into remarkably soft-hearted grandparents. As we reflect on our own journey, we admit that we, too, have been reformed in this role. As the saying goes, "Grandchildren are the dots that connect the lines from generation to generation." Without this phase in our lives, we would have missed the immense joy of watching him grow, the warmth of shared experiences, and the deepening of our family bonds. It was a leap of faith, a joyful step forward that beautifully filled the missing pieces of our lives, reminding us of just how precious and fleeting these moments truly are.

Then came the killjoy, COVID-19, like an unexpected storm that reshaped our lives in ways we could never have anticipated. It quickly disrupted our daily routines and severed connections, particularly with loved ones who were far away. For many of us, it meant missing out on precious moments with our children and grandchildren.

Those two years felt like an eternity, a significant chunk of time lost. Milestones that once would have been celebrated together were now observed through screens. Video calls and messages became our lifeline, but no virtual connection could replace the warmth of a hug or the joy of shared laughter. The isolation created a palpable sense of distance, leaving us yearning for the simple comforts of togetherness—a family gathering, a spontaneous outing, or even a quiet moment shared with loved ones.

Each missed birthday, anniversary, and festival was a reminder of the precious moments slipping away. We watched growth and change unfold through pixels, longing for the real experience of being together. The home-bound reality was wearing on us, and so, in a moment of defiance, we accepted an invitation to a Christmas party in December 2020. Desperate for a break from the prolonged isolation, we booked a four-night stay at a hotel for the New Year weekend, not knowing the storm it would bring. By early January 2021, my husband tested positive for COVID-19, and I soon followed suit. The virus knocked us down completely.

What truly pulled us through was our younger daughter, who stayed with us during the worst of it. Despite the personal risk, she put aside her own family to care for us, showing an extraordinary amount of love and sacrifice. We are profoundly grateful for her unwavering support. Her selflessness was a reminder of the strength of family, and it made us truly count our blessings during such a challenging time.

In the midst of our struggle, we learned to adapt. We found new ways to celebrate and stay connected, even though the emotional weight of those two years lingered long after. The pandemic taught us about the fragility of time and the importance of cherishing every moment.

As the lockdown was lifted, life slowly returned to a semblance of normalcy. Yet, the health setbacks faced by so many seniors could never be fully undone. What mattered most was our resilience, and the deep gratitude we felt for simply being alive—the chance to cherish the company of our children and grandchildren. Too many, both young and elderly, didn't make it through this period.

Reflecting on it all, we realize how essential it is to recognize the clarity that comes from such experiences, to cherish each new day, and to hold onto the gratitude we now carry for the moments we still have. We made it through, and that alone is something to be deeply thankful for.

CHAPTER NINE

Passions unleashed

In quiet moments, when the rush subsides
Forgotten words awaken, no longer denied.
Notebooks wait, their pages bare
Ready for stories, ready to share

Pen meets paper, thoughts pour free
A journey shaped by joy and agony
Every moment a canvas, every sunset a dream
Crafting a life more than it may seem.

#Passion 1

**Writing*

I found solace in words from a young age, my notebooks filled with stories and poems, each page a canvas for my imagination. The act of writing offered me a refuge, a way to shape my thoughts and emotions into something tangible. I was fortunate to have teachers who guided me in writing using imagination rather than following any prescribed style. Their encouragement and praise—especially when accompanied by good grades—ignited a spark of confidence within me. Each compliment felt like a small affirmation of my ability, but my father's feedback truly impacted me. When he read through my scribbles, his simple comment— "promising... keep writing"—became a guiding light, propelling me forward in my pursuit of writing.

From an early age, I was also a passionate reader. Books were my constant companions, each one expanding my vocabulary and deepening my understanding of the world. I often found myself drawn to stories that transported me to different places and times, fuelling my desire to create. Reading broadened my perspective, giving me a treasure trove of experiences and voices that shaped my writing. The rhythm and flow of language became as natural to me as breathing, and I soon discovered that writing, like reading, had the power to connect me to something larger than myself.

Small victories in school competitions further encouraged my growth. Though very modest, these achievements served as an impetus to keep writing. However, it was in the workplace that my passion for writing truly blossomed. When asked by the Head of the Branch office to edit his book, it felt truly rewarding, like a significant milestone...a tacit admission of my skills and potential. His generosity in crediting me in the acknowledgements was a moment of pride and his book, "Management of Sales Territory", published in 1996, still occupies a proud place on my bookshelf, serving as a 'forever' reminder of my journey as a writer.

Beyond personal accomplishments, the opportunity to help others with their writing brought me immense satisfaction. Colleagues would often seek my assistance with their work and I found joy in refining their ideas, offering feedback and helping their voices shine. It was a collaborative spirit that deepened my appreciation for writing as a tool for connection and empowerment. Knowing that my support could help someone else succeed was a powerful motivator and it reinforced my belief that writing is not only a means of personal expression but also a way to uplift others.

As my career progressed, writing took on new dimensions and purposes. After two decades in the professional world, I found myself preparing for MBA exams, where academic writing and assignments became my primary focus. This period reshaped my relationship with writing, pushing me to refine my voice and communicate complex ideas with clarity and precision. It was a time of growth, where professional writing flourished in ways I had not anticipated.

However, life's journey is seldom linear. The responsibilities of being a wife, mother, caretaker, and active community member eventually demanded a shift in my priorities. While these roles were deeply fulfilling, they also required me to reimagine my engagement with writing, following a different set of requirements. Drafting resumes for neighbours, and sending proposals to embassies for immigration on behalf of those seeking jobs overseas, became a satisfying hobby during this lull in my creative life. But despite these quieter moments, the foundation I had built over the years remained steadfast. Writing was no longer just an activity but a passion—an intrinsic part of who I was. Even when temporarily sidelined, it evolved in the background, patiently waiting for its next chapter.

Through all phases of my life, writing has been a constant companion. It has helped me process thoughts, share experiences, and connect with others. More than a skill, it became a tool for personal growth and empowerment. Each chapter of life has brought new challenges and opportunities, deepening my relationship with the written word. With every turn, writing has grown richer and more meaningful, continuing to be a vital thread that weaves through my story.

Once my responsibilities began to ease, I found myself in a unique space where time seemed to pause, nudging me to start writing. It all began in 2015 with contributions to online forums on Facebook and various writing platforms that invited writers to share their thoughts in response to daily prompts. I found immense joy in this—writing spontaneously, straight from the heart, during breaks from my daily chores.

Encouraged by my husband, I published my first book of poems, "Evocative Renderings", in 2017. As an aspiring writer, I approached its release with modest expectations—perhaps a small footprint in the writing community. While the book didn't achieve significant recognition, it didn't deter me. The following year, I released "Tales of the Twins", a collection of prose poetry that didn't fare well either, largely due to marketing oversights by the publishing house. I took it in my stride, reminding myself that this was merely part of the journey.

The pandemic brought its challenges, particularly for children who faced isolation and upheaval. Motivated by empathy, I penned stories and poems for young readers during this turbulent time, culminating in "Minds Unplugged: Lockdown Stories and Rhymes for Six to Sixteen", published in 2021. Though it vanished quickly from view, I learned that success isn't solely defined by sales or accolades. My passion for writing remained steadfast.

In 2023, I released *Trail Mix*, a collection of short stories crafted to resonate with diverse perspectives. This time, the publishing model was unique, providing me with fifty copies to share directly. While its overall reception remains unknown, I was thrilled to receive a few heartwarming reviews from fellow writers whose opinions I deeply value.

Watching many talented friends—often from academic backgrounds—achieve remarkable milestones with multiple publications has been inspiring. Their success reflects their dedication and determination, and I couldn't be happier for them. My own journey as a writer has followed a different path—slower, less conventional, and sometimes uncertain—but it has been deeply fulfilling. I've embraced each step with gratitude, cherishing the growth and learning that have come along the way.

Alongside the rise of self-publishing, new opportunities began to emerge for me to contribute to anthologies, both in India and abroad. Though my efforts were humble in comparison to the impressive works I saw around me, I approached each opportunity with enthusiasm and a quiet eagerness. Like a schoolgirl seeking inclusion, I submitted my stories and poems to these collections, hoping they might find a place among more established voices. The joy I felt when my work was accepted was truly humbling—each acceptance, no matter how small, felt like a personal victory.

However, in my eagerness, I often lacked the organization to properly track the various anthologies where my work had been featured. Some of these collections now grace my library, cherished as reminders of those milestones, but there are others I never managed to obtain copies of, leaving me with little more than the memory of my small contributions. I recognize now that while my presence in these anthologies might not have turned heads or met the lofty expectations of the wider writing world, each publication held a special place in my heart. They were the quiet affirmations of my journey, not measured by the fame of the anthology or the recognition of my name, but by the simple act of having written and shared a part of myself with others.

Reflecting on my journey, I find the hashtag #writer doesn't quite capture my experience. You might wonder why, and I would say it's because I don't see myself as a born writer, a cultivated one, or even a professional. Now in my seventies, I still hesitate to label myself as a writer in the conventional sense. My writing journey has been unplanned and uncharted, arising from a unique blend of factors that have allowed me to express myself through words.

Writing, for me, is more than just a means of communication; it is an enabling tool that opens up worlds of understanding and connection. Each word becomes a bridge, linking my innermost thoughts to the broader tapestry of human experience. In a society often marked by noise and haste, writing provides a sanctuary where I can pause, reflect, and distil my thoughts into something tangible. It's an act of creation, a way to shape the chaos of my mind into clarity.

What gives me immense satisfaction is not just the act of writing itself, but the knowledge that my words sometimes resonate with others. I find a deep sense of purpose in articulating the complexities of life and in exploring the nuances of our shared experiences. Writing allows me to confront the maladies of society—inequality, injustice, the struggles of the marginalized—and to delve into these issues with a critical eye. It empowers me to ask difficult questions and challenge prevailing narratives.

Through writing, I've been able to document not only my reflections but also the larger societal issues that weigh heavily on my heart. It becomes a form of advocacy, a way to amplify voices that are often silenced. I write not just for myself but for those who feel unheard, who grapple with their own stories in a world that can feel dismissive and overwhelming.

In this journey, I've discovered that vulnerability can be a powerful tool. Sharing my own struggles, fears, and observations invites others to connect with my experiences on a deeper level. It fosters empathy and understanding, reminding us that we are not alone in our challenges. Writing has allowed me to weave a narrative that reflects both personal and collective journeys, highlighting the threads that bind us together as human beings.

As I continue to explore this path, I realize that writing is not about achieving a certain status or fitting into a specific mould. It's about embracing the act of expression, revelling in the joy of storytelling, and remaining open to the lessons that emerge from my thoughts. Whether it's a poignant reflection on ageing, a critique of societal norms, or a celebration of resilience, each piece becomes a testament to the power of words.

The recognition I've received, though a bit later in life than I might have expected, has been a humbling and meaningful experience. Being nominated for the 2024 Pushcart Prize for Poetry and having my work accepted into respected anthologies feels like a gracious validation of the path I've quietly followed. These moments of acknowledgement remind me that the worth of one's work isn't measured by accolades or timing but by the sincerity of the effort and the honesty of expression. The recognition is a kind gift, but I know the true reward lies in the ongoing writing process, in each poem and each line that helps me better understand myself and the world around me.

In this light, I see writing as a lifelong companion, one that continues to evolve alongside me. It challenges me to think critically, observe the world with intent, and seek meaning in the ordinary. Ultimately, it is through this uncharted journey of writing that I find my voice, not as a conventional writer but as a seeker of truth and a storyteller in my own *right. I realize: "**I am not defined by labels, but by the words I weave through life.**"*

#Passion 2

**Travelling: A Love Affair with the Unknown*

My love for adventure is deeply rooted in my DNA, a quirky inheritance from my *Thakurma* (grandmother) and Baba. While they were drawn to spirituality and seeking answers to life's cosmic mysteries—far beyond the excitement of a simple road trip—my journey is a bit different. For me, travel is a way to immerse myself in the beauty of new sights and sounds, to experience diverse cultures, and to savour the unique cuisines of different countries. This deep fascination with exploring the world eventually led me to study geography and geology, allowing me to combine my passion for adventure with a deeper understanding of the places I visit. Travel, for me, is not just about seeing new landscapes, but about connecting with the world in a way that enriches my soul and broadens my perspective.

My earliest travel memories go back to the weekend jaunts with Baba, Ma and my siblings—our pet tagging along, of course. We ventured to newly opened resorts along the Damodar Valley, graduating with epic road trips to Ranchi, Varanasi and a memorable train ride to the seaside haven of Puri. Each holiday was a fresh wave of excitement, fuelled by Baba's infectious enthusiasm and his delightful "don't care" attitude when ordering the best meals at hotel stays. The result? A whirlwind of binge eating, the occasional stomachache, frayed tempers, and plenty of sightseeing—every moment utterly unforgettable.

Travelling became a cornerstone of my academic life as well, as I pursued my geography degree. I found myself trekking to remote areas, all the way to Jawai Bandh in Rajasthan, where under the guidance of our professors, we gathered/collated data for the thesis project. Shorter road trips to study rock formations in the Damodar Valley were livened up by the presence of our teaching staff and Nuns, who accompanied us on our bus adventures. I can't help but chuckle at the mischievous memories that bubble up—like those hilarious stops in the Sal forests when we all had to answer nature's call. I still wonder how the Nuns, swathed in layers of fabric, managed to handle it with the same level of grace we did. The looks of relief on their faces? Priceless.

Then came the fateful day when I met my travel soulmate. The universe must have had a giggle because we shared a profound love for adventure. He had already trekked across the USA, Canada, Europe, and Russia—essentially three-fourths of the globe—during his student backpacking days while returning home from post-graduate studies in Canada. Sharing his travel tales, flipping through his photo albums, and watching his slides stoked my wanderlust even more.

Our first trip together was a bold move right after our wedding: a honeymoon in Darjeeling, which raised more than a few eyebrows for going against tradition. But who could extinguish our rebellious spark? Not even the prospect of impending parenthood could keep us grounded. By their first birthdays, our little ones were already travelling with us—exploring beaches and hill stations and visiting grandparents on our annual escapades. Family vacations became a ritual during their growing-up years with their aunt and uncle accompanying us. Occasionally, we made it an 'only girls' vacation, with Ma, the girls, and us siblings, dashing off to the seaside, the temple town of Tirupati, to the hill station in Ooty, creating memories exclusive to us... of the mishaps, funny moments, near accidents...we as the women brigade successfully navigated.

Relocating to a new city opened a world of travel opportunities, particularly in the beautiful southern regions of the country. Our adventures began with spontaneous road trips to serene jungle resorts along the banks of the Cauvery River, as well as exciting excursions with friends, to the picturesque hill stations of Kodaikanal and Ooty, and the vibrant sea-side destinations of Goa, Pondicherry, and Trivandrum. One of the highlights was taking the girls on their first overseas trip to the UK in 1998, which I believe marked a significant milestone in their growth and learning experiences.

Overseas travels began in earnest in 1991 when I started accompanying my husband on work-related trips. These excursions allowed us to explore various countries together, including Canada and the USA from coast to coast, the UK and parts of Europe. Though our stays were often brief, they offered us cherished 'couple time' away from the hustle of everyday life.

Between 2000 and 2010, while our children pursued their studies and careers in the USA, we made it a tradition to visit them every year. These trips were often spontaneous, driven by any excuse to travel. It was only starting 2012, that our leisure travel took off on a massive scale. We explored European countries, Southeast Asia, and Japan, often returning to revisit places we hadn't fully explored on previous trips.

Each journey we undertook was meticulously planned with my husband leading the charge and organizing every detail. Initially, we relied on travel agents, but we quickly realized that their rigid schedules left us feeling rushed and exhausted. This prompted us to embrace independent travel, where we could set our own pace, choose our accommodations and savour local cuisine at our leisure.

Not that our newfound freedom wasn't without its challenges. We made our fair share of mistakes along the way, often misjudging hotel locations, leading to inconvenient stays far from the attractions we wanted to explore. Delaying in booking sightseeing tours came with the heavy price of missing out on highly sought-after experiences. Each misstep brought its brand of disappointment, serving as a harsh reminder of the importance of careful planning.

In due course, we learnt that travel is often filled with unexpected challenges that can disrupt even the best-laid plans. No matter how seasoned or intrepid a traveller may be, there are always incidents that can't be anticipated—like the time we were mugged in a foreign country. What followed was a string of frustrating and time-consuming events that seemed to multiply our sense of helplessness.

This unsettling experience unfolded in Athens when we became victims of a quick-handed pickpocket on the subway. In a matter of seconds, my husband's wallet was gone, leaving us stunned and disoriented. But that wasn't the end of it—our pickpockets were efficient. They had also dipped into my sling bag and made off with my wallet too. The suddenness and audacity of it all left us reeling, with an overwhelming sense of violation.

What followed was an exhausting and frustrating ordeal that drained both our patience and energy. Our first stop was a shabby, poorly lit police station, where we waited for what felt like an eternity for an officer who seemed reluctant to even acknowledge our complaint. His indifferent attitude only deepened our sense of helplessness. After what seemed like endless back-and-forth, we were told to head to the Tourist Police Office to officially file a complaint—more waiting, more red tape. Then came the international calls. We spent over two hours on the phone with our bank and credit card companies. Each call was a painfully long-drawn-out process of verifying our identities before instructing them to cancel the stolen cards. By the end of it, we were both mentally and physically drained.

In the grand scheme of things, the financial damage was minimal—a few notes of cash and the hassle of replacing a couple of cards. But the emotional toll was much greater. The excitement of our trip had quickly been overshadowed by the frustration of being robbed and the overwhelming series of steps needed to mitigate the damage. What should have been a simple resolution turned into a relentless and draining ordeal, one that left us feeling defeated and disillusioned! The experience served as a stark reminder of how unpredictable and challenging travel can be, even when you think you've prepared for the unexpected.

During our visit to Cambodia in 2014, an unexpected incident added an unplanned twist to our eagerly anticipated sunrise experience at the magnificent Angkor Wat Temple. This iconic view draws millions of visitors, all gathering by the lake to watch the sky transform into a golden masterpiece, with the temple's reflection shimmering in the water.

In my excitement to capture this breathtaking scene, I underestimated the dew-soaked terrain beneath my feet. Morning dew, as it turns out, is not just picturesque—it's also deceptively slippery. One misstep was all it took. At that moment, I felt like a clumsy dolphin attempting a graceful dive but instead starring in an impromptu slapstick routine.

The grand finale? I landed flat on the ground, trading a perfect sunrise photo for three fractured ribs and an intimate new relationship with pain I definitely hadn't signed up for.

Despite this setback, I was determined not to let it overshadow my trip. With the help of painkillers and trusted Volini ointment, I soldiered on, albeit with the grace of a wounded gazelle. This experience highlighted a crucial lesson for us: the true test of resilience lies in how we face the unexpected.

This brush with danger heightened our awareness in future travels. We became more vigilant, adapting our approach to prioritize safety without compromising our sense of adventure. Each journey thereafter was not just a chance to explore new places but also an opportunity to learn from our past, turning misfortune into wisdom and resilience.

The balance of good and bad has often played out in unexpected ways during travels and our visit to Japan was no exception. One morning, to my dismay, I discovered that an earring was missing from my left earlobe. A thorough search—under the bed, across the carpet, in the washroom, and every other conceivable spot—yielded nothing. The nagging thought crept in: *Was this a bad omen?* Still, we pushed it aside and set out to enjoy the day's itinerary, immersing ourselves in the breathtaking beauty of the landscape.

As the day unfolded, the incident slowly faded from my mind, overshadowed by the wonders we were experiencing. When we returned to the hotel, exhausted, I was more than ready to crawl into the freshly made bed, turned down for the night. As I flicked on the night lamp, ready to settle in, something caught my eye—a shiny object resting on the paper coaster on the nightstand.

I couldn't believe it. There, in plain sight, was the missing earring. It was as though time had rewound itself and placed it back in my path. I surmised that the housekeeping staff must have found it and carefully placed it there for me. It was a moment that filled me with both gratitude and surprise. In an industry where mistakes can easily be overlooked or mishandled, this simple act of honesty was a reminder that integrity still thrives.

When people ask what's left to see, we remind them we've only ticked off five out of seven continents—two more still await! Our goal is simple: to explore every single one while our legs still work and our energy doesn't require a mid-afternoon nap.

Despite being septuagenarians, our desire to learn, explore, and enjoy the world remains vibrant. We are driven by an insatiable wanderlust, a travel fever that shows no signs of diminishing. Every new destination ignites our curiosity, and each experience enriches our lives. We find joy in the stories, cultures, and landscapes that await us, proving that the spirit of adventure knows no age.

For those like us, bitten by the travel bug, there's a deep-seated need to see the world—an unyielding passion that compels us to pack our bags and embark on new adventures, no matter where the journey takes us.

So here we are, navigating the world, one adventure at a time, and we wouldn't have it any other way! As we look to the future, we remain eager to embrace every opportunity for exploration. Each journey holds the promise of discoveries, enriching our lives and deepening our connections with the world around us. Whether it's wandering through ancient streets, savouring local delicacies, or engaging with diverse cultures, we believe that travel is a lifelong pursuit that transcends age. Our hearts are full of anticipation for the adventures that lie ahead, as we continue to chase our dreams and feed our wanderlust. After all, the world is vast, and our journey is far from over.

Travel writing began for me when mobile phones became ubiquitous. I've always avoided taking my laptop on trips; the hassle of security checks—pulling it out, repacking it and the constant worry of dropping it—just felt too cumbersome. Initially, I relied on my iPad to jot down notes. However, that strategy came to an abrupt end when my iPad met its fate after slipping from my hands onto a sidewalk in Barcelona. Before I could even reach for it, a horse-drawn carriage filled with enthusiastic tourists finished the job.

Now, my faithful mobile phone is my primary tool for documenting my travel experiences. I write whenever I have a moment—waiting in airport lounges, on flights, or just before I go to bed. This practice ensures I don't forget the names of foreign places or historical sites, and it allows me to capture the emotions of my journey in real time. I've recorded these reflections on my WordPress blog, where I share both the joys and the challenges of my adventures.

Travel writing is more than just a personal record; it's a way to connect with others and inspire them to explore the world. Through my experiences—both the triumphs and the mishaps—I hope to convey the richness of travel and the lessons learned along the way.

CHAPTER TEN

Brush with Celebrities

In the quiet dusk of a life well-spent
I gather memories, where time has lent
A tapestry woven with joy and strife
Each thread, a story, a glimpse of life

With silvered hair and wisdom's grace,
I pen the laughter, the love, the chase
For those who read, may they find their way
In echoes of yesterday, where dreams still sway
A memoir is more than just words on a page

The journey of seven decades has not been without its share of encounters with celebrities, both big and small. Some left a lasting impression, while others faded into the background like a fleeting star. Some of these encounters are unforgettable, as their charisma, talent, or presence resonated deeply, influencing the course of my thoughts or emotions. These individuals have become part of my personal story, forever etched in memory. Both kinds of encounters remind me of the fleeting nature of fame and the people who shape it.

A throwback to 1956-57 (thereabouts): The first notable encounter was at school with the famous Tagore sisters, Sharmila and Oindrilla, popularly known by their pet names, Rinku and Tinku Tagore, distant relatives of Guru Rabindranath Tagore through their parents. It was a brief crossing of paths at Loreto Convent, Asansol. At the time, the younger sister, Tinku, had already achieved stardom with her role in *Kabuliwala* as the young Mini. The film was screened in our school assembly hall while she was still the fair, chubby, curly-haired student, a few years senior. Sharmila, the elder one, a discovery of Satyajit Ray, made her mark in Tollywood later, with her performance in *Apur Sansar*, catapulting her to fame. I vaguely remember the petite Rinku, with two long braids and the school belt tightly cinched around her narrow waist, chatting with her classmates. Her beauty and lineage made her a subject of whispered admiration. But it wasn't all glamour. The nuns at school frowned upon acting and as Rinku confessed, she was told to leave. As her career soared, we followed her rise and eventual shift to Bollywood.

My next celebrity encounter came in 1963-64 when I met *Puluda* (Soumitra Chatterjee), the hero of *Apur Sansar* and many of Satyajit Ray's films. Whenever he was on an outdoor shoot near the *Maithon/Panchet* Dams along the *Damodar River*, he'd drop in to visit his childhood friend, *Soumnenda* (a neighbour). On one such visit, we had the opportunity to meet him, following an alert call from the neighbour. My twin and I scrambled downstairs, hair uncombed and mouths full of biscuit crumbs, eager to meet the iconic actor. His screen presence did little justice to the person I met up close—tall, handsome, and unassuming—nothing like the larger-than-life persona I had imagined. After some small talk, he recited a poem in his sonorous voice, leaving us in awe. His parting words, "*Abar dekha hobe*" (we'll meet again), were unforgettable. And sure enough, I saw him again years later at *Soumenda* and *Rinadi's* firstborn's rice ceremony in Calcutta, where he continued to be humble and approachable.

During my college years, from 1969 to 1972, children of celebrities joined, left, and got married. Prominent among them was *Moon Moon Sen*, the late Bengali heroine Suchitra Sen's daughter. What made her endearing to others was her simplicity and her striking resemblance to her mother. There was also a Miss India runner-up, a Miss Calcutta and children from famous industrialist families.

Later, I met a few more notable figures. In 1976, I crossed paths with Pritish Nandy, a literary figure and close friend of my husband. In 1977, when he received the Padma Shri, we attended the party celebrating his award. His sense of humour, turning even the mundane into delightful anecdotes, made him the life of the party. In 1978, when we were tenants in his house, we met some of his writer friends. I remember him as down-to-earth, even when surrounded by fame. A multi-faceted personality passes away, a little too early, just as I write about him. The literary and cinematic world will miss him as much as his friends who have seen his meteoric rise.

In the corporate world, I had the privilege of working with Ajay Banga, now President of the World Bank. As Branch Manager at Nestlé in Calcutta in 1989, he was the epitome of an empathetic leader—approachable, participative, and genuinely respected by his staff. His leadership style was a model for all.

During my husband's long stint with UB Group, I often met Vijay Mallya, the "King of Good Times." First at his wedding reception in Calcutta, where he and his wife Sakina, greeted each guest personally—a rarity among ultra-rich families. His parties, always star-studded, became the talk of the town and I had the chance to attend several, to find the 'who's who' of the industry, celebrities, movie stars and pop singers, in attendance. Mallya had a knack for hosting the best parties, making every event feel like a grand celebration.

Looking back, my encounters with celebrities were defined not by their glamour but by their humility and down-to-earth personalities. Even as the years have passed, these memories remain vivid, leaving behind more than fleeting interactions with famous faces.

On an entirely different and profoundly rewarding plane was the opportunity to meet and interact personally with His Holiness the Dalai Lama—not once, but twice.

The first occasion was in 2004, at a small, private gathering where each attendee was photographed with Him. A photograph of Him, holding our hands, now hangs framed on the wall—a constant reminder of the extraordinary blessing we received. In that brief yet profound hand-holding, we felt something otherworldly, as though drawn into the radiance of His spirituality and magnetism, which seemed to form an almost tangible aura around Him.

The second meeting took place in 2019, in McLeod Ganj, Dharamshala, His present residence. Though the toll of age and declining health was apparent, the light in His eyes remained undimmed. When He greeted me with a firm handclasp, the strength in that touch carried the same transformative energy—a transmission of spirituality that has stayed with me ever since.

These encounters remain among the most cherished moments of my life, leaving an indelible imprint of His Holiness's grace and luminous presence.

Celebrity encounters, though often fleeting, have a lasting impact on us. They can inspire us, reminding us of the heights one can reach through talent, hard work, and dedication. But they can also teach us humility, showing us, that fame is often just a moment in time, and that beneath the public persona, many of these individuals are just like anyone else—human, approachable and fallible. The positive influence of celebrities can be profound, but it is equally important to recognize that the allure of fame can also bring with it pressures and distortions, making it a double-edged sword. In the end, it is the humility and kindness of those we meet, whether famous or not, that leave the most lasting impressions.

Reflections: A Memoir of Simplicity

In a world that often celebrates grand achievements and lofty status, I have found contentment in the quiet embrace of the ordinary. My life has not been defined by monumental triumphs or public accolades. Instead, it has unfolded like a gentle stream, meandering through the landscape of everyday existence. As I reflect on my journey through these memoirs, I hope to offer a sincere testament to the profound beauty found in the mundane moments that often go unnoticed. Even the smallest experiences carry deep significance, and it is through these quiet reflections that I have come to understand what it means to live fully and authentically.

I grew up in a small town, where the rhythm of life was governed by the seasons and the subtle changes in the air. My parents, spiritual and hardworking individuals, taught me the value of diligence and perseverance—not for recognition, but for the satisfaction of living a meaningful life. They instilled in me the belief that fulfilment does not always come from external accolades, but from the warmth of home, the laughter shared with friends, and the simple joys of life.

As I moved into adulthood, I embraced the roles of daughter, friend, partner, and eventually, mother. Each role brought its challenges and joys, though none were marked by a spotlight. I watched some of my peers achieve extraordinary heights—becoming doctors, artists, and entrepreneurs—while I found peace in the small victories: earning my MBA in my forties, preparing a meal with love, sharing heartfelt conversations with my partner about retirement, and authoring books. These moments, simple as they were, were rich with meaning.

There were days when I felt the weight of comparison, questioning whether my life was "enough." But as I began to document my memories, I realized that even the smallest moments held immense value. A rainy afternoon spent with my children, listening to their chatter over fried *onion pakoras* (fritters), the quiet companionship of a friend over coffee, the weekly movie outings with my mother, the simple act of watching the sunset with my partner—each of these experiences wove together to create a tapestry rich in meaning. I discovered that my story, though not extraordinary in the traditional sense, was inherently human. It encapsulated the shared experiences of many—moments of doubt, joy, and resilience. I learned that there is strength in vulnerability and power in authenticity. In embracing the ordinary, I have found peace in the realization that true fulfilment lies not in outward success, but in the daily acts of love and intention.

As I look back over seven decades, it is not the major milestones that stand out most, but the subtler moments—the spaces between the events, the small joys, and the quiet revelations that often went unnoticed in the hustle of living. Time has softened the sharp edges of both joy and sorrow, revealing a deeper understanding of what truly matters. I've come to realize that life is not about what we accumulate—whether memories, accolades, or possessions—but about what we give away: love, wisdom, and kindness. The people we've touched, the fleeting connections, and the enduring bonds—these are the true markers of a life well-lived.

At seventy, I find peace in the knowledge that we are never finished growing, no matter our age. There is always more to learn, more to experience, and more love to give. I have learned that the greatest peace comes not from achieving a list of goals, but from surrendering to the present moment, trusting the process, and finding grace in every step of the journey.

I have also discovered that beyond life's earthly rhythms, spiritual leanings have brought me profound peace. Through prayer, reflection, and a quiet connection to something greater than myself, I've come to understand that my life is part of a much larger tapestry—a divine design that unfolds beyond the visible. It is through this spiritual peace that I have learned to navigate challenges with grace, embrace the imperfections of life, and surrender my need for control. In this trust, I have found an inner balance and a deeper sense of belonging.

Being a grandparent has added a beautiful new dimension to my life. It has reignited my desire to live longer and to witness the next generation thrive in a world that often values external success over inner peace. I hope to impart the wisdom I've gained along the way, offer guidance as they navigate their paths, and support them with love and kindness. And at the end of the day, I feel immense gratitude for the love I've given and received, and for the ordinary moments that have made my life so richly fulfilling.

As I close this chapter, I do so with deep gratitude for the years I've lived, the people I've met, and the lessons I've learned. I move forward not with expectations, but with an open heart, ready for whatever the future brings. Life, I've come to realize, is not a destination but a journey—shaped by each step, choice, and moment of connection. Thank you for sharing some of these steps with me, and to all those who tell their stories, enriching our collective experience.

Writing this memoir has been a profound act of self-reflection. It has allowed me to see my life not as a series of isolated events but as a continuous thread of experiences, each with its own meaning. In writing, I have been able to distil the essence of my journey, uncovering lessons I may have overlooked in the rush of living. I hope that by sharing these reflections, I can offer something of value—perhaps an insight or a moment of recognition—to anyone who reads it. In telling my story, I realize that it is not just my story, but part of a much larger shared human experience. Writing my memoir has reminded me that the purpose of life is not just to live, but to leave behind a trace of love, wisdom, and meaning for others to find. As Euripides wisely said, "The best and safest thing is to keep a balance in your life, acknowledging the great powers around us and within us. If you can do this, you are truly wise.

My journey can be summed up with the following:

Born in the Cradle of the 50s

Born in the cradle of the 50s,
I carry the weight of two centuries—
the whispers of post-war lullabies
and the clang of millennial alerts

I grew up with radios crooning golden tunes,
only to grow old with playlists in my pockets
I flipped through typewriter ribbons,
banged the carriage back in place
and punched holes in stencils—

bringing words alive in black ink

These hands that once turned rotary dials
also washed soiled cloth nappies
Shaped like Doritos—triangular, of course
Now these same fingers swipe screens
with a precision even my younger self
would applaud

Oh, yes, I danced to Elvis,
swayed to disco,
and now Google how to sync
my hearing aids with Bluetooth
Once, I marvelled at black-and-white movies;
now I grumble when Netflix buffers.

"I'm vintage, not old—
like wine, but cheaper!"
And behind the humour lies a depth
that might just crack open hearts:
a world where letters flowed from fountain pens,
and patience wasn't a lost virtue

I am a warrior of change,
with bifocals perched like crowns
I carry the stories of my grandparents,
and the dreams of my grandchildren.

Sure, I fumble with tech at times,
but my wisdom downloads instantly—
proof that the past and present
can co-exist in a waltz
that never skips a beat.

- *Snigdha Agrawal*

About The Author

Snigdha Agrawal (née Banerjee) is a lifelong learner navigating the ever-evolving world of writing. Her cosmopolitan upbringing has shaped her unique voice, blending Eastern and Western cultural influences in her work. A graduate of Loreto Institutions, she brings insights from two decades in the corporate world to her storytelling, exploring genres like short stories and poetry. Based in Bangalore, she shares her travel experiences on her blog, capturing the essence of new places and cultures. Now in her 70s, Snigdha continues to embrace life with curiosity, drawing strength from her nearly fifty-year journey with her husband. Through her writing, she hopes to connect with readers, share stories, and leave a small, meaningful impact.

www.ingramcontent.com/pod-product-compliance
Lightning Source LLC
LaVergne TN
LVHW021153160826
845679LV00024B/2111